D1570296

Scientism and Education

Emery J. Hyslop-Margison • M. Ayaz Naseem
Authors

Scientism and Education

Empirical Research as Neo-Liberal Ideology

 Springer

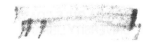

Emery J. Hyslop-Margison
University of New Brunswick
Fredericton
Canada

M. Ayaz Naseem
Concordia University
Montreal
Canada

Library of Congress Control Number: 2007935891

ISBN-13: 978-1-4020-6677-1   e-ISBN-13: 978-1-4020-6678-8

Printed on acid-free paper.

9 8 7 6 5 4 3 2 1

springer.com

Dedication

Dr. Kieran Egan, an exceptional mentor and scholar, whose academic work has been a tremendous inspiration

Foreword

We presently live in an era dominated by scientism, an ideology that believes that science (and its rationalist foundation in modern epistemology) has an undeniable primacy over all other ways of seeing and understanding life and the world, including more humanistic, mythical, spiritual, and artistic interpretations. In being critical of scientism as I am, I am not against science per se: modern science and its ways of understanding and knowing the world are valuable, and we should be grateful for them. But it is the hegemony of the habits of mind that manifest pervasively in education that privilege science education, career, and research over other modes and branches of learning and knowing that I have problems with. I have too often witnessed parents overtly or subtly discouraging their children from following artistic or humanistic aspirations and pushing them for training and careers in Science, Math, Business, and Technology. In this society we say in a thousand and one ways that money, security, power, and ultimately fulfillment reside in these disciplines and not in the Arts, Humanities, and Philosophy. We valorize scientists, and even when they speak on subjects outside their domain of expertise, we take their opinions and pronouncements as definitively authoritative. When Science speaks, people listen.

This hegemonic attitude towards Science and other subjects that require the exercise of our rational and intellectual faculty is reflected in educational research as well. In the pantheon of educational research, empirical research deals with the tangible and observable, and hence can count, measure, and predict sitting at the throne and command the largest funding and unequivocal respect, whereas research in Arts and Humanities, which propose to, or actually do, inspire, edify, and in general call for transformation of moral or social consciousness and appeal to conscience, is often ignored, neglected, and perhaps even worse, trivialized and dismissed. This devaluing and dismissive view of educational research that is not characterized by data collecting, counting, measuring, and predicting permeates the graduate classrooms of educational research courses, and by extension, the whole of graduate students' academic culture.

As an illustration, I recently taught a graduate-level educational research course in which students were introduced to the distinction between quantitative and qualitative research with the view that these students have to decide what kind of research they would do for their theses and dissertations. What was so very fascinating to me was just how much of the discussion in class had to do with students' worries and fears over the vulnerable image of qualitative (especially the conceptual) research and researchers. They were all nervous about the image of "fluffy stuff" and "flaky people" attached to research and researchers that do not deal with quantifiable and measurable data. Indeed, they had great concerns about the "image" of conceptual, phenomenological, hermeneutical, or arts-based research. Indeed, in retrospect (with 20/20 hindsight), I would say that the major (unintended) curriculum for this course turned out to be critical epistemology that helped students understand where this devaluation of *quality* came from, and why we privilege empirical research modeled after the "hard" sciences over and above other kinds. If we say that hard sciences and the like are where money and power is, then we have not explained anything at all: it becomes a circular argument.

The rise of modern science was the epochal phenomenon of seventeenth-century Europe. And the impetus behind it was apparently noble and humanistic: to free humanity from cycles of war, oppression, poverty, and disease that plagued feudal Europe, by unfettering their minds from religious fundamentalism, ideological dogmatism, and superstition, with the aim of improving humans' material conditions through science and technology. Indeed, they needed such liberation rather badly, and we still do, today. Science, the champion of humans' rational faculty for logic and observation, was to be the liberator of humanity. The European Enlightenment folks were convinced that with Science, we could combat all human ills – mental, physical, or social. We no longer needed to be helpless and at the mercy of forces and powers, natural and otherwise. We can control Nature, Life, the World, and control outcomes in the ways that we want. Unfortunately, things do not always work out the way they were originally conceived and intended, and in retrospect, we come to see in clearer light what went, and is going, so terribly wrong. To repeat, hindsight tends to be more accurate than foresight. So what went wrong with the scientific and technological revolution that started in the seventeenth century and is still unfolding?

Based on my research over the last decade, the seeds of trouble were there from the beginning of modern science, and in fact go back to the beginning of western civilization when Plato and his contemporaries despised the senses and privileged rational intellect. In fact, some theorists have made a case that the trouble goes even further back, to the beginnings of agriculture when humanity abandoned the hunter-gatherer's life and began to plow the land, which was interpreted by some as the first radical act of violence against the Earth. At any rate, this is not the place for a detailed historical tracing about this fascinating topic. What I wish to address in this foreword, by way of lending a support to Hyslop-Margison and Naseem's critical stance against the prevailing trend in educational research, is an understanding of scientism and its damaging manifestations and implications. For that, I wish to contribute a brief analysis of scientism against the backdrop of the inception of modern science and the misguided visions and hopes that surrounded its birth.

At the heart of modern science and the rise of empirical research is the understanding and aspiration that humans can shape their own destiny, rather than be fatalistically dependent on external powers, be they God, Deities, Destiny, the underlying Logos of the universe, or any other names emerging from different cultures. The idea was that by learning to think for themselves they could make their own informed decisions, and gain increased control over their lives in the process. These are laudable aspirations. Yet, within these aspirations were contained erroneous understandings that led the modern world astray and impact directly on our contemporary fetish for scientific methods in education research. Then as now, binary and dualistic thinking grips and cripples us. In wishing to grow out of dependence on external powers, such as God or Fate, we (collectively speaking) ran towards the dichotomous opposite – independence, which ended up creating the current egotistic, competitive, control-oriented, individualist cultures. Focusing on human power, we began to neglect and forget the more-than-human dimensions of Being, notably, the ecosphere. We became narrowly and even blindly humanistic, materialistic, and subsequently disconnected from the Earth, Heaven, and the Intangible and the Immeasurable. In recognizing how we went astray, and the associated deep suffering that comes from the resulting existential disconnection or alienation, many are now reacting against the materialist, individualist, and secular cultures we created, and are militantly pushing for rebuilding a theocentric world order with God in charge. (And of course, there are ongoing bloody battles over whose God should be in charge.) As Anthony Giddens has observed, the rise and spread of fundamentalism with its associated conflict and violence globally is possibly the greatest challenge we are facing today. To note, fundamentalism is not confined to religion: it is a mental outlook that insists on authoritarian control and dogmatic adherence to one "right" set of beliefs and values. As such, fundamentalism applies to all spheres of human values, beliefs, and practices, including educational research. At its root, then, scientism is a form of fundamentalism.

At the heart of fundamentalism is binary or dualistic thinking that sees the world in terms of "either–or," "for-or-against," "right or wrong," "black or white," and so on. To counter fundamentalism in any substantial way, it is this dualistic thinking and the associated mental habit of privileging of one side and devaluing the other that we need to deconstruct and overcome. Dualistic habits of thought have us think in terms of dichotomous binaries. We are set up to think in terms of either dependence (heteronomy) or independence (autonomy), reason or emotion, intellect or senses, fact or value/taste, secular or sacred, quantitative or qualitative, and so on, wherein one side of the binary is superior to the other. We need to abandon the binary logic of *either–or*, and embrace the integrative logic of *both–and*. In the consciousness of *both–and*, the dualism between autonomy and heteronomy gives away to the perception and understanding of interdependence or mutuality. Likewise for all other binaries. The opposite pairs (e.g., dependence and independence) integrate, and give rise to the *third kind* (e.g., interdependence). In terms of educating human beings, we need to nurture intellect *and* senses, reason *and* emotion, logic *and* intuition, and integrate them so that each pair is truly integrated rather than a war zone that leaves the casualties, psychically crippled individuals. This cultural shift, however, is far easier said than done.

It is extremely difficult to abandon dualistic thinking and binary choices because, having internalized the societal norms and values from the earliest moment, we have already learnt to devalue one worldview and privilege the other. In our culture and civilization, we prioritize reason over emotion, logic over intuition, intellect over senses, and so on. Hence, individuals are socialized to repress emotion, intuition, senses, and the like. This is, I suspect, how my graduate students have come to see "fluffyness" and "flakeyness," rather than "sensitivity" and "responsiveness," in qualitative research. That schooling is intimately and massively involved in this repression is not a state secret. On the contrary, it is part of the mandated curriculum and pedagogy. Well meaning and caring as they are, teachers, being the products of this society and culture that devalue emotion, intuition, and senses, end up "teaching," wittingly and unwittingly, repression of these capacities. Subtly and not so subtly, every day, students receive the message that to be truly successful in this society, they have to devalue and underdevelop emotion, intuition, and the senses. These are "fluffs" that "flaky" people like. No wonder, then, that my graduate students are anxious and nervous about qualitative research. And when they choose to take that path, they become anxiety-ridden about doing it "right." In their anxious effort to ensure its "legitimacy," they are driven to look for guaranteed "recipes" for successfully completing their qualitative research! How ironic, if not downright absurd. By its very definition, is not "quality" something that eludes outwardly tangible and externally validated criteria?

Each society defines its terms of success: what counts as success, and who are deemed to be "winners." Ours valorizes and promotes competition, winning, success, aggressive strength, control, penetrating intellect, *hard* facts, *rigid* standards, quantity, measurement: all to do with the tangible and the measurable. All of these are what are known as "masculine" values or attributes. (In Chinese thought, *yang* is equivalent to "masculine" attributes, but *yang* does not have a gender denotation, which is the reason why I like to use this terminology.) Again, these values or qualities per se are not really problems. We in fact need them, but in moderation and generously balanced by the "feminine" (*yin*) modes and values, such as receptivity, sensitivity, humility, flow, flexibility, resonance, empathy, compassion, caring, and the like. (To note, ideally, both males and females embody a balance of *yin* and *yang* qualities. No gender stereotyping here.) These *yin* qualities, in contrast to the *yang* qualities, are intangible, immeasurable, uncontrollable, unpredictable, unaccountable, or in the Daoist Chinese vocabulary, mysterious (*miao*). When these polar (not dichotomous) qualities come into balance and integrate, the following social dynamics are more likely to appear: cooperation, harmony, and peace. But when the *yin* qualities are devalued and marginalized, and the *yang* qualities in excess, as in the present times, what we see in the culture is rampant greed blindly dominating, exploiting, and consuming. When greed is predominant, the society and its citizens go "mad." Our activity of turning the Earth into a human waste sink and committing ecocide is categorical madness. The world's war zones where nations, tribes, citizens, neighbours, and fellow students bomb, shoot, stab, and torture each other is another sign of this madness. Given the state of the world, what ought to be the mission of education? Should we in education perpetuate the state of imbalance and madness by continuing to marginalize the *yin* or so-called feminine values and practices? Should we not as educators critically re-examine the very definition of success and the society's dominant patterns of de/valuation?

But to live in a culture dominated by hard and aggressive masculine *yang* values is precisely to be prejudiced against the "fluffy" and "flaky" (i.e., as seen from the dominant value perspective) *feminine* values. Thus, the first crucial step we need to take to begin to address this prejudice is making visible what the dominant patterns of thought (aka, ideologies) are, how they came about, and how they play out in various arenas, including the academy and its minefield called "research." I am very pleased to see this crucial and critical step taken in this book by Hyslop-Margison and Naseem. They reveal in fine, even if quite painful, detail, neo-liberalism and its ideology of aggressive, market-driven capitalistic success, and how it impacts educational theory, research, and practice, marginalizing the yin in the process. They convincingly show the intimate connection between neo-liberalism and the hegemony of empirical research and are to be congratulated for their efforts. This is an important book and one that, at the very least, should begin a conversation about how we can strike a more even balance in education between focusing on the rationalism of science and addressing the foundational questions so critical to resolving the most troubling issues of our times.

Vancouver, BC   Heesoon Bai
June 2007

Acknowledgements

First, we acknowledge the permission of *Theory and Research in Social Education* to reprint excerpts from A Critical Examination of Empirical Research: The Case of Citizenship Education, Volume 34, (3) and permission from the *Journal of Curriculum Theorizing* to reprint excerpts from "Scientism as Neo-liberal Ideology: The Fallacy of Objectivity in Educational Research, Volume 21 (4).

There are many people whom we would like to thank for helping with the completion and production of this book. First and foremost, we express our thanks to the University of New Brunswick and Concordia University for offering unmitigated support to our scholarship.

We also offer our profound thanks to Heesoon Bai from Simon Fraser University who wrote the thoughtful and compelling foreword for this book. We would also like to formally acknowledge the research assistance of Adrian McKerracher who copy-edited the manuscript and provided extremely helpful suggestions for revision. We also owe a debt of gratitude to Harmen van Paradijs, our editor at Springer Publishing, for his support during the writing and publishing process.

Last but not least, of course, we owe an incalculable debt to our families for their ongoing support and patience. We send our love and unending thanks, for without you our work would have far less meaning.

Contents

Authors

Dr. Emery Hyslop-Margison is an Associate Professor in the Faculty of Education at the University of New Brunswick in Fredericton, Canada. He has published extensively in areas of democratic learning, philosophy of education, and work studies, and recently held a Canada Research Chair at Concordia University in Montreal, Canada. He is also past Director of the Institute for Democratic Learning in Career Education.

Dr. Ayaz Naseem is an Assistant Professor in the Department of Education at Concordia University in Montreal, Canada. His research interests include feminist theory and philosophy, post-structuralism, diversity in classroom, peace education, democratic, and citizenship education.

Chapter 1
Introduction

The Present Context of Empirical Research in Education

The entire discipline of education as a legitimate field of academic study is at a virtual crossroads. One path leads to the same unfortunate errors that have sullied education and educational research for more than 150 years. This well-trodden path, laden with a range of ideological assumptions and epistemological mistakes, generates instrumental forms of thinking and learning that operate to undermine the critical dispositions required for meaningful education within democratic societies. The other path, which we believe to be the far more enlightened choice, understands the limits of empirical research and emphasizes instead the purposes, goals, and strategies of education within democratic societies.

This second and far more progressive path seeks to develop innovative pedagogical ideas and theories that understand learning strategies as following logically from educational objectives. As Dewey (1916) so accurately pointed out, the means and ends of education are intrinsically connected. In other words, our approach to instruction is embodied in the type of education we seek to achieve. Empirical research, therefore, becomes virtually superfluous and an unnecessary drain on the severely limited resources available to schools, teachers, and administrators. Our more favoured path creates students who are politically informed and active participants in shaping their social, economic, occupational, and political experiences. Hence, the stakes that have compelled us to write this book are enormously high for both the future of teacher education and for education as an academic discipline, as well as for democratic societies more generally.

Obviously, our decision to write this book was not a responsibility or challenge we took lightly with regard to its potential impact on the relationships we treasure with our academic friends and colleagues. We therefore appeal to them not to take our critique personally, but to view it as an opportunity to stimulate productive dialogue and debate. We fully appreciate, even respect, the intellectual investment many of our colleagues have in the empirical work they carry out, and we admire both their work ethic and their professional dedication. For the most part, they are serious academic scholars, committed to their profession, and they pursue their scholarly work with the complete conviction that they are "doing science" and, in the process, they believe they are promoting the interests of teacher education, schools, and students.

In spite of generally good intentions, often lost within academics under layers of personal ambition, career building, promotion and tenure, and credential acquisition, we argue herein that education researchers are in fact achieving none of the above. Unfortunately, researchers are instead piling up considerable amounts of circumstantial evidence that is far too weak or conclusive to form any concrete foundation for educational policy development. Educational research is simply distracting our attention from the real issues undermining quality learning such as social class disparity and dwindling financial resources. From an ideological perspective, researchers are also promoting instrumental rationality in education, and pursuing neo-liberal and human capital precepts that reduce teachers and students to objects being crushed under the burgeoning weight of neo-liberal globalization and its corresponding labour market demands.

In a recent article that appeared in the *Teachers College Record*, McClintock (2007) offered a critical appraisal of contemporary research in the field of education. He argued, quite compellingly, that research in the field has essentially become little more than a growth industry that generates, in the final analysis, more confusion among teachers and academics than reliable strategies for sound educational practice. He describes the American Educational Research Association's (2001) recently produced *Handbook of Research on Teaching* as follows:

> It epitomizes thousands of person-years of methodological inquiry, each piece of it fine fare, but in bulk indigestible. It assembles work, pointless in a deep existential sense, for the research goes off in every direction, leaving those in practice, policy, school administration, teaching, instruction, and parenting without a clue what to do. Before them, a research landscape spreads out, a vast plain, with a hillock here and there among the dead (Dewey, Freire, Piaget, and Vygotsky) and the living (Shulman, Darling-Hammond, and a few others). Because educational researchers have proven unable to exercise rigorous control and account for the relevant variables in carefully designed inquiries, their studies have had notoriously conflicting results. If researchers cannot master the variables in controlled settings, why expect practitioners, caught in institutional cross-currents and daily coping with complexity, to be able to rationalize school activities according to the prescripts of research findings? (McClintock, 2007, p. 1)

In his brief but powerful critique, McClintock suggests that education research has little to do with what occurs in schools but is, contrary to the widespread rhetoric, doing a significant amount of actual harm:

- Skill in educational research often has little to do with the real educational work that should take place in the professional preparation of educators. By relying on the demonstration of extraneous research skills as the prime criterion of recruitment, promotion, and tenure, schools of education risk making bad decisions about the composition of their faculties.
- School improvement requires quotidian labour, many persons thinking hard on their feet, responding to an endless flux of concrete situations with knowledge, care, and insight. The myth that fixing the schools somehow depends on the magic of educational researchers deflects attention, material support, and respect from those charged with the real tasks of keeping school, diminishing their morale and confidence.

- By working primarily to secure their recruitment, promotion, and tenure, educational researchers become alienated and defensive. They avoid intellectual risks; they become imitative; they seek narrow, predictable specialities; they address a limited readership and nurture small ideas that others will find unexceptional. In so doing, they educate themselves poorly and as poorly educated educators, they prove impotent as the educators of educators (p. 2).

At the risk of portraying ourselves as academic heretics in our field, we believe the situation in education research is, in some ways, even worse than McClintock describes.

The journey to arrive at this point in the history of education research has been a long one marked by a persistently poor reputation among members of the scholarly community. Faculties of education, at least since Dewey, have been marginalized by the general academic community as having no legitimate place within the university environment. Although we do not subscribe to this particular view, we do believe that dramatic changes are required in the work performed by faculties of education if we are to dig ourselves out of the deep hole in which we find ourselves.

The view that science and the scientific method provides the mechanisms to strengthen public education arguably began with the futile and now even embarrassing claims of British philosopher Herbert Spencer. In spite of his early failures and rather inane ideas (at least many of them seem inane to us in a contemporary sense), the view that science affords researchers with the appropriate tools to improve education continues to gain astonishing momentum. For example, the American Educational Research Association's (AERA) recently published *Handbook* referred to by McClintock weighs in at 7 lb and includes just less than 1,300 pages of printed text. To say the least, it is a lot of material, much of it overtly contradictory in its claims, for both researchers and teachers to digest.

We wish to make clear from the beginning of this book that our complaint in the following pages is not with science in the main. Indeed, we believe science is an effective investigative tool when applied to appropriate subject matter – subjects such as chemistry, physics, and biology. Of course, even natural science has its issues, both theoretical and practical. The problems created by natural science and technology in areas such as climate change are coming home to roost but that problem, and others, is more one of application than the result of a fundamental incommensurability between method and subject matter as is the case with education. Our overarching concern expressed herein is that human beings generally and education in particular do not provide appropriate domains or subject matter for the employment of meaningful scientific inquiry.

Since many of the distinctions are virtually self-evident, there is no need to enumerate at great length the range of differences between the subjects of study in natural science and human science. Our rather basic point, one we will reiterate throughout the forthcoming pages is that human beings are dynamic sorts of creatures. We are, at times, highly unpredictable, and most importantly of all, possess something referred to as *agency* or *freewill*. Many of our colleagues in the physics department might suggest that agency is simply an illusion and that, in fact, human actions are as predetermined as every other material force in the universe. Hence, it would follow that if we could identify the appropriate scientific method or protocols, we could understand and predict the course of human action in the manner sought by the human sciences. Indeed, it is this tacit materialist assumption standing behind much of the research conducted in education. However, there are at least three fundamental problems with this position.

First, the position of *determinism* – that human actions are causally determined by antecedent forces that can be identified and manipulated – makes absolutely no sense in relation to our lived experience. Whether it is an illusion or not we make thousands of intentional decisions and choices on a daily basis that influence the direction and quality of our lives. Second, the *determinism* that results from a mechanistic worldview is a metaphysical claim that evades the very standards of science employed to either verify or falsify scientific statements. Although one may claim humans lack freewill or agency based on materialist assumptions, such a claim can never qualify as a legitimate proposition – as a statement that may be demonstrated definitively as true or false – and therefore such claims fall beyond the domain of science. Third, even if human experience is determined in a scientific and causal sense, the calculations required to explain and predict human behaviour would be so complex that they are obviously beyond the realm of human understanding and identification. In spite of statisticians' methods suggesting the contrary, the number of possible variables is almost indeterminate given human complexity. Hence, it makes no scientific or pragmatic sense to discuss our existence in the deterministic or mechanistic terms necessary to identify axiomatic pedagogical principles. When considered collectively, these three reasons alone significantly undermine the notion that a human science of education is remotely possible.

In this book, then, we hope to demonstrate that the attempt to apply logical positivist principles to the study of education is counterproductive to strengthening teaching and learning practices, drains the limited resources that target education and reproduces the human capital precepts underlying schooling within a neo-liberal context. By targeting micro-level actions and behaviours, education researchers select the incorrect unit of analysis to actually improve the quality of education for all learners. We argue instead that democratic societies must finally confront the serious economic inequalities that actually generate the disparate learning outcomes existing within contemporary education rather than continue to be misled by an ideological smokescreen of empirical research. Policymakers and government funding agencies must recognize that limited available resources require the proper targeting of funds both at the level of schools, but also, and perhaps even more importantly, at the level of addressing social disparities. Tinkering with classroom practice will never resolve the impact of social and economic inequality on student academic achievement.

The causes for the rise of empirical research in education are varied and complex, and are rooted in both an instrumental view of education as a technical enterprise, and a misguided faith in science, borne in *Enlightenment* optimism, as a panacea to all human problem solving. In spite of the ubiquitous popularity of empirical research in education, as we have pointed out above, its actual reputation among the scientific and academic communities is quite another matter. Kaestle (1993) observes, for example, following interviews with 33 educational researchers and federal agency officials, that education research has "an awful reputation" (p. 136). There is little to no evidence, he concludes, indicating that empirical research generates any improvements in education practice. The reason for this disconnect is often blamed on the lack of implementation of research findings or the limited impact of research on teacher education. However, we are convinced that the problem is far more fundamental since the actual rupture between research and education occurs at the level of the applied method and how it fails to connect with the subject matter in question.

Since the late nineteenth century when education was first established as a scientific field of inquiry most notably through the work of Herbert Spencer, controversy has ensued regarding the tenability of viewing education as a *scientific* problem. Education research has been long contested on the basis of two primary criticisms: first, there exists the view that the very possibility of research and expertise in education is suspect given the contested and normative nature of the field (Egan, 2002). Without specific ends in mind, the methods to achieve any chosen objective are always subject to normative critique; second, there are the serious methodological and epistemological issues, many of which we discuss in the following pages, that raise fundamental questions about the possibility of even doing educational research. Lagemann (1999) summarizes this latter problem as follows:

> Among those engaged in education research, there have been, and continue to be, constant charges and counter charges concerning the merits of different methods, findings and problem statements. At least among educational researchers the dance is well known. Leaving aside differences derived from differing roles and professional identities, more often than not studies of the same problem reach fundamentally different conclusions. For every study in education research, there are an equal number of opposing studies. Charges and counter charges among people engaged in education research reduce the credibility of the enterprise and make it difficult to find common ground. (p. 8)

Perhaps we are overly sanguine in our aspirations (life is always somewhat easier when one adopts an optimistic outlook about things), but we genuinely hope this book mounts a significant challenge to the empirical research paradigm in education and that we bring more immediate closure to its otherwise painful and protracted demise. Indeed, we have virtually "studied" education to death and the time is long overdue to act appropriately in a moral fashion to improve the general accessibility to quality academic experiences.

Empirical research will not repair decaying schools in urban areas, improve social disparity, raise teachers' salaries or assist communities suffering from widespread drug and alcohol abuse. The resolution of these problems depends on proper moral decision-making and a political framework committed to social and economic equality for all citizens. As we point out in the text that follows, we already possess the required knowledge and resources, when appropriately channelled, to correct or at least reduce these problems. What we sadly lack, however, is the political and moral will to transform that knowledge into political, social, and, ultimately, educational action. Until that will is developed, with due respect to those conducting such studies, all of the empirical research cited in the AERA's *Handbook* will have a negligible impact on improving the general quality of education.

1.1   Chapter Preview

In Chapter 2, we explore the history of human science from its early influences and inception to its present application. These early influences include the work of seminal figures such as Francis Bacon, Auguste Comte, and, perhaps most importantly and directly for education, the British philosopher and scientist Herbert Spencer. This chapter also maps out the fundamental tenets of logical positivism and offers a preliminary analysis of the corresponding epistemological problems in applying these principles to education. We also discuss the implications of existential and pragmatist philosophies for empirical research in education, and introduce the current socio-political context of scientism as the prevailing ideology influencing educational research.

   In Chapter 3, we examine the problem of how scientific theories are subject to numerous conceptual and theoretical commitments, and are supplemented by various ad hoc principles that protect these theories from falsification in Popper's sense and, hence, remove their related claims from the domain of genuine science. We explore Karl Popper's theory of falsification in some depth, one now typically viewed as the gold standard of scientific legitimacy. We also examine the assumptions of structuralism by reviewing in detail the positions of sociologists Emile Durkheim and Lucienne Levy-Bruhl. We outline the strengths and weaknesses of the structuralist position and discuss the theory's implications for education research, and for understanding education as a socio-cultural phenomenon. We also introduce Thomas Kuhn's concept of scientific paradigms and explore its implications for research in education. In sum, this chapter deals another considerable blow to the notion that a *science* of education is remotely possible.

   In Chapter 4, we explore in far greater detail the impact of value judgements on empirical research in education by addressing the problem of researcher and normative bias. In particular, we will examine the supposed empirical claims of such documents as the No Child Left Behind legislation in the USA and other similar policy initiatives. These programmes typically and incorrectly identify such issues as incompetent teachers and unacceptable levels of student achievement as problems that can be resolved through empirical forms of research and measurement. To the contrary, we reveal that a range of serious epistemological and philosophical problems beset the empirically based systems employed to assess teachers and students.

   In Chapter 4 we also investigate the conceptual confusion and ambiguity that exist in education research, and consider the implications of this problem for research outcomes. We explore how a tacit commitment to the direct reference theory of language influences empirical research in education. This chapter illustrates how two or more researchers, adopting different normative or theoretical assumptions/frameworks, while employing the same rigorous empirical methods of inquiry, may nonetheless reach radically different conclusions when investigating identical educational phenomena. In part, this observation explains why there are so many competing claims within education regarding similar educational practices.

The limited applicability of educational research in actual classroom situations is obviously a point of serious concern throughout this text. Why would we bother to conduct extensive and resource draining empirical research if there was not the attending hope of achieving at least some major improvements to teaching and learning? Past and present critiques on this subject, however, have raised grave and trenchant concerns about whether empirical research in education is achieving anything more than analytic or trivial truths about teaching and learning. Put another way, the implications for classroom practice that emerge from educational research simply advance definitions of ordinary language concepts related to education. In Chapter 5, we explore this potentially damning critique in some detail and discuss how it affects fields of study such as democratic citizenship education. This chapter also examines and debunks through this same critical lens empirical claims about what constitutes best practice in teaching.

The proponents of empirical research in education advance their positivist and socially reproductive agenda by presently dictating what counts as meaningful educational research. As the recent AERA manual on education research suggests, the movement continues to gain professional and ideological momentum in spite of a paucity of meaningful results. In Chapter 6, we argue that the only real solution to redress the problem of low student academic achievement and attainment requires meeting the moral imperatives of social justice and equality of opportunity within democratic societies.

In order to actually change the quality of education for all students, educational researchers and teacher education faculties must move beyond misguided empirical practices that merely deflect attention from actual schooling problems and instead become part of the political struggle for the fairer distribution of economic resources within our societies. By exposing the technical weaknesses and ideological implications of empirical research in education, this book ultimately offers radical dissent to the ideological hegemony of educational scientism. Its ultimate aim is to shift research and discourse in education towards more human studies and toward more morally focused and successful methods of educational inquiry.

Chapter 2
Education Research

History and Context

2.1 Introduction

In this chapter, we explore the development of scientism in education by examining the advancement of human science through the work of seminal figures such as David Hume, Sir Francis Bacon, Auguste Comte, and Herbert Spencer. We also introduce the foundational principles on which empirical research in education is based by reviewing the basic tenets of logical positivism, the epistemology on which human science is constructed.

There is some belief that the shift toward more qualitative research practices undermines the stranglehold that logical positivism holds over education research. In response to this belief, we examine in Chapter 2 whether postpositivist research paradigms and practices constitute an actual departure from positivist assumptions. After briefly discussing the philosophical critiques of human science emerging from existentialism and pragmatism, we conclude the chapter by outlining the current neo-liberal context in which education research and policy development take place.

The pervasive nature of empirical research in education and its present hegemonic status is only too obvious among those of us who reflect on the current context of our work. For example, one of us recently received a manuscript returned from a major Canadian education journal indicating that although the work was being accepted, somewhat reluctantly, for publication, the editor and one reviewer from the four experts consulted maintained the piece did not qualify as "research" because it lacked an experimental design. The related allegation from the editor suggested that the manuscript was an "opinion piece," and we might assume of course it was an opinion he felt disinclined to accept. However, as good fortune would have it, the peer review gods that oversaw our academic fate smiled upon us, and the editor succumbed to the concerted pressure from the two supporting reviewers to accept the article.

Although we share this tale with some sense of irony, there is a serious message conveyed by this story because education research is largely driven by the promotion and tenure process of academic institutions. If you want tenure, the message conveyed in the subtext of institutional discourse is to avoid scholarly controversy in favour of compliance by strictly obeying hegemonic forms of research practice. Such behaviour may make for successful academic politics, but it affords a negligible outcome to improve education and schools and, in our case, would represent personal intellectual dishonesty.

The article we refer to actually reviews a range of curricular documents from the Canadian province of Ontario containing career-related literacy components and critiques these documents via a democratic learning framework. This type of research/scholarship falls within the category of policy analysis, an approach that openly reveals and justifies its normative assumptions in advance of the forthcoming analysis, and evaluates policy in light of these adopted values. We mention this particular article and situation at the beginning of this chapter only because it highlights the academic dogma within contemporary education regarding what counts as scholarship and research, and how resisting scientism potentially impacts deleteriously on academic careers.

Allegations regularly fly in faculties of education concerning scholarship quality, and the question "where's the empirical evidence?" gets repeatedly asked, oddly even when one is discussing normative issues or philosophical questions. Many researchers in education have seemingly never heard of the fact/value distinction let alone understand that it inevitably defines the limit of legitimate empirical inquiry and distinguishes science from scientism. Questions of value such as what constitutes a quality education, what defines quality teaching, or what constitutes intelligence or giftedness for that matter, simply cannot be resolved through empirical study, a basic fact to which many of our colleagues and friends in educational psychology remain seemingly and dangerously oblivious.

To suggest there are vested interests in protecting empirical research in education from serious scholarly critique would be an understatement of considerable magnitude. When one of us began a mission to question the value of empirical research in education he was warned by a senior mentor, respected colleague and internationally established scholar to "watch your back." This warning was recently borne out at one of our recent tenure hearings when our challenge against empirical research quickly became the focus of the committee meeting rather than the overall quality of the submitted tenure dossier. We enter this discussion, then, with the full realization that we are treading on very dangerous and hallowed ground.

Needless to say, our colleagues who do empirical work are somewhat less than enthusiastic about this book. But we fully anticipated that reaction. After all, careers, research journals, conferences, research centres, and entire departments and faculties of education are built around the notion that empirical study will eventually deliver education to some type of pedagogical promise land, a teaching and learning Utopia so to speak.

Unfortunately for our colleagues devoted to empirical practice, the track record of empirical research in education paints a somewhat bleaker and more pessimistic picture, a portrait of enduring stagnation and, quite sadly, mostly abject failure in improving classroom practice. Hence, we are forced to conclude that something or some things are terribly amiss when it comes to applying empirical methods to education. Somewhat ironically, the empirical proof for our controversial claim sits solidly in the pudding of long-standing failure.

The incentive to write this book, then, emerges from a compelling need to finally draw a proverbial line in the sand and mount the professional and intellectual courage to state what is becoming increasingly obvious to many. The "problems" of education, teaching and learning simply do not lend themselves to empirically based resolution. Indeed, a critical exploration of the history of social science research might have suggested this outcome to empirical researchers long before we decided to craft this book, but it is a history that many of our colleagues have apparently not heard or perhaps do not want to hear. As we pointed out in the introduction, we also want to make it abundantly clear from the beginning that this book is not an attack on science per se, but rather on its dogmatic application to education as the only acceptable or productive research paradigm.

It is initially important to understand how education as a discipline of inquiry arrived historically at its present position regarding research. From where did this unbridled faith in science as a panacea to virtually all human problems emerge? The faith in science and the scientific method was initially and sanguinely adopted almost 200 years ago by Auguste Comte who viewed empiricism as the ideal vehicle to resolve all problems besetting human experience. Comte's overly optimistic faith in empiricism is relatively easy to understand. Indeed, science was initially a liberator from prevailing dogmas and from religion's long reigning monopoly over what counted as knowledge in the seventeenth and eighteenth centuries. However, the ideology of scientism has become the reigning epistemological tyrant.

It is worth citing Feyerabend (1975) at some length here to elucidate the tremendous influence scientism enjoys over our contemporary world and how it has replaced religion as the prevailing dogma, situating itself as beyond meaningful challenge or critique:

> Scientific 'facts' are taught at a very early age and in the same manner in which religious 'facts' were taught only a century ago. There is no attempt to waken the critical abilities of the pupil so that he [sic] may be able to see things in perspective. At the universities the situation is even worse, for indoctrination is here carried out in a much more systematic manner. Criticism is not entirely absent. Society, for example, and its institutions, are criticized most severely and often most unfairly and this already at the elementary school level. But science is excerpted from criticism. In society at large the judgment of the scientist is received with the same reverence as the judgment of bishops and cardinals was accepted not too long ago. Pursue this investigation further and you will see that science has now become as oppressive as the ideologies it once had to fight. (p. 5)

Indeed, as Feyerabend suggests, there was a time when science held great promise as an emancipating force from the stranglehold of religious dogma and the various forms of oppression it promoted. Over the last 200 years, this confidence has been transformed into an ideology completely blind to the limits of empirical study, and employed, we argue, to protect the interests of the ruling elite.

Although we will revisit the subject later in this chapter, we wish to draw a clear and immediate distinction between science and the scientism so prevalent in education that we reject. Scientism is an ideological position that champions the methods of natural sciences above all other modes of human inquiry. It embraces only empiricism and inductive reasoning to explain any and all elements of human experience regardless of their derivation. We employ the term scientism in an entirely pejorative sense because it involves an attempt to apply scientific practices in contexts where they are methodologically inappropriate and ideologically manipulative. The over commitment to science results in both epistemological distortions, many of which we describe in this text, and bad public policy in education and elsewhere. Scientism, then, is an ideological rather than epistemological movement that results in a range of negative effects on schooling.

2.2 The History of Empirical Research in Education

Deeply concerned with what he saw as the reasoning and epistemological errors of his epoch, in the seventeenth century, Sir Francis Bacon (1963) crafted the *Novum Organum*. This seminal work in the development of modern science and the scientific method was written to dispel what Bacon considered an enduring and misguided faith in metaphysics and formal, or deductive, logic as absolutely reliable epistemological instruments. His concern over the misuse of formal logic was extremely well founded. For centuries, as he correctly observed, the ancient instruments of Aristotelian logic undermined the scientific search for new and reliable knowledge by supporting various outrageous claims on the basis of argument validity. Aristotelian logic promoted numerous metaphysical claims, primarily religious ones through the Scholastics, and misguided beliefs as immutable truth "proved" through the logic of deductive validity.

In the thirteenth century, for example, Thomas Aquinas (1951), a seminal figure in the development of formal Catholicism, employed Aristotelian deductive logic to "prove," through valid argument structure, God's existence in five different ways. Of course, what was really at question within each of Aquinas's five proofs was not the validity of the arguments (as Bacon later pointed out, absurdities can be easily proved as valid through deductive or formal logic) but rather the soundness or truth of the premises on which these proofs were based.

To his credit, Bacon recognized the seemingly simple point that argument validity affords no assurance of argument truth and that the premises of any argument must be verified by observational, or empirical, and inductive means to offer some measure of epistemic certainty. Validity is a necessary condition of argument truth but not a sufficient one. In the absence of the premises being subject to empirical and inductive verification, the arguments simply encourage additional metaphysical confusion by deductively proving false or at least highly dubious metaphysical conclusions. As Bacon reflectively observed:

> The logic now in use serves to fix and give stability to the errors that have their foundation in commonly received notions rather than to help the search after truth. So it does more harm than good. The syllogism consists of propositions, propositions consist of words, and words are symbols of notions. Therefore if the notions themselves (which is the root of the matter) are confused and over-hastily abstracted from the facts, there can be no firmness in the superstructure. Our only hope therefore lies in true induction. (Bacon, 1963, p. 187)

In place of the deductive reason introduced by Aristotle, then, with these prophetic words Bacon proposed the general application of empirical verification and inductive reasoning, or impartial observation and inference, the rudiments of scientific inquiry, as the most reliable means to identify truth. The *Novum Organum* began the initial and critically important shift from unwarranted and often spectacular metaphysical claims toward the principles of modern day science.

There can be no doubt that Bacon's contribution to natural science was a much needed step that steered philosophical inquiry regarding the nature of things in the proper epistemological direction. However, as we demonstrate later in this text, even such unquestioned confidence in induction, inference, and explanation presents science with a different set of difficulties. Although the approach developed by Bacon typically works very well within natural science, its application to the study of humans and human interaction such as classroom outcomes remains highly problematic.

Since Bacon, of course, natural science has enjoyed exceptional progress with many dramatic discoveries such as those by Galileo, Newton, and Einstein all resulting in major paradigm shifts, and thereby changing how we understand and describe the world around us. We have traveled to the moon, sent space probes to the furthest reaches of our solar system and beyond, and uncovered many of the DNA mysteries surrounding human illness and life itself. We have developed amazing technologies in virtually every area of human experience as we learn more and more about the origins of the universe and about the development of life on Earth. We are able to speak and communicate via cell phones and the Internet with individuals on the farthest reaches of our planet with unbelievable speed and facility. In combination, natural science and its progeny, technology, have dramatically changed the very nature of human experience and will undoubtedly continue to generate a tremendous impact on the kinds of lives our children lead in the future. The clock on science cannot and should not be turned back, but we must also recognize where and when the scientific method is applicable and effective, and where and when it is not.

Although a comprehensive discussion of the issue is beyond the scope of the present text, we would be remiss not to at least point out that the impact of natural science and technology on human experience has been far from uniformly positive. Indeed, in spite of our respect for science, we have no particular scientific fetish. As a result of burgeoning technological development, we confront extremely troubling issues such as global warming, poisoning levels of air pollution and clean-water shortages that place our entire planet and its biological population in peril. An objective analysis of natural science inevitably leads to the conclusion that it has been at best a mixed blessing to our lived experience by offering both hope for a better life but often at an unforeseen or frequently ignored environmental and human cost.

Recently deceased and respected academic in education Neil Postman (1988) used the automobile as a classic example to drive home the point that science is not a necessary good. On the one hand, we have tremendous ease of mobility, now being able to travel vast distances on modern highways in comfortable vehicles with relative ease. On the other hand, the environmental cost of fossil fuel combustion is staggering, as is the annual death toll on our public highways. Similarly, the nuclear technology we have developed can be used for peaceful means in medical diagnoses, or far more darkly for the virtual destruction of human civilization. Generally, however, we cannot deny that the steady advance of natural science has drawn us closer and closer to understanding more about the world we all share. That observation, it seems to us, is an entirely unproblematic claim.

Whereas the progress of natural science and the technologies it produces has been dramatic if not necessarily environmentally friendly, the social sciences, especially in education, continue to struggle, rather unsuccessfully we argue herein, to gain even some small measure of scientific credibility. In spite of an initial faith that it could deliver the goods, social science has failed quite miserably at solving the most serious human problems we face, including widespread moral corruption as evidenced by examples such as the Enron fiasco, the recent Liberal Government corruption scandal in Canada, and the Abu Ghraib atrocities committed by US troops in Iraq to mention only a few.

The type of problems we enumerate above, similar to many of the ones confronted in education, are not empirical problems. They are deeply moral, or normative, problems and on that front our progress has been almost non-existent. Our technological tools have become far more sophisticated but actual instances of sustained moral progress, although perhaps not entirely invisible, are far more difficult to identify. Science will never be able to provide the sought after solutions to these problems regardless of the sophisticated methods and analyses employed. As a related observation, we might add that while our fascination with science as a research method has increased in education, the actual time spent on genuine moral education and moral dialogue with students has correspondingly decreased.

The mountains of empirical research established at the level of classroom experience, as we pointed out earlier, have failed to produce tangible improvements within education (Egan, 2002; McClintock, 2007). Although our empirically based research colleagues would no doubt disagree, the progress in education at the hands of empirical research is, and we are being somewhat charitable, negligible at best. To anyone understanding the obvious epistemological distinctions between knowledge about humans and knowledge about things, this failure was, of course, highly predictable.

There are many factors that influence the study of education such as its normative nature, virtually infinite classroom variables and, perhaps most importantly of all, human agency, all factors that studies in natural science simply do not confront. Nevertheless, the attempt to apply scientific principles to the study of humans and human behaviour, especially in the field of education, the demand that we perform "research" as our aforementioned editor contends, continues to gain momentum in spite of the accumulating counter evidence regarding its positive influence on teaching and/or learning outcomes.

The view that science and empirical methods provide the best available means to improve education is partially rooted in the nineteenth-century perspectives emerging from both Auguste Comte's unbridled faith in human science and philosopher

Herbert Spencer's development of what are best described as pseudoscientific principles of learning. Comte's (1974) contribution to the increased influence of science was profound and he is often described as the founder of the positivist movement in social science and philosophy (Stump, 1989).

Comte ignored Hume's (2000) previous warning regarding the possible construction of a social or human science. The latter's faith in developing such a science that could accurately understand and predict human behaviour ended in virtually complete and publicly self-admitted failure. Indeed, Hume's early faith in the promise of developing a human science eventually led him to a radical scepticism about the possibility that any such endeavour could achieve even a small measure of success. His early faith that a science of man could be established is nicely captured in the following narrative:

> We must glean from our experiments…from a cautious observation of human life, and take them as they appear in the common course of the world, by men's behaviour in company, in affairs and in their pleasures. Where experiments of this kind are judiciously collected and compared, we may hope to establish on them a science, which will not be inferior in certainty, and will be much superior in utility to any other form of human comprehension. (Cited in Laird, 1967, p. 23)

It did not take very long before Hume's radical empiricism eventually led him to some rather unanticipated conclusions, especially regarding the possibility of a coherent and predictable self, a fundamental requirement of a tenable human science. In the absence of such prediction, a human science in any meaningful sense is impossible.

If humans were little more than bundles of spontaneous sensations, as Hume concluded in his analysis of the self, then the idea of identifying predictable human patterns of behaviour was obviously a seriously misguided one. Without a stable and predictable self, accurately predicting human behaviour through axiomatic principles either collectively or individually was impossible and knowledge in any meaningful sense, Hume concluded, was therefore necessarily limited to analytic propositions and natural science. As Hume (2000) observed following his abandonment of human science as an epistemological possibility, "It seems to me, that only matters of the abstract sciences or of demonstration of quantity and number [qualify as knowledge], and that all attempts to extend this more perfect species of knowledge beyond these bounds are mere sophistry and illusion" (p. 121). As we demonstrate in the following chapters, this sophistry and illusion still accounts for most of what is termed scientific research within education.

As much as perhaps we might like to lay the entire blame for the current situation on the doorstep of the current Bush administration and its preoccupation with protecting neo-liberal ideology from criticism, such an accusation ignores the last 150 years of history in education. The stage for the present debacle we confront was set far earlier in the development of human science and to understand that story we return to the work of August Comte.

In the nineteenth century, Comte's (1974) primary and clearly overambitious objective for a new brand of all-encompassing positivism, an obvious precursor to contemporary scientism, included the complete reorganization of civil society. In his view, the promise of the Scientific Revolution that followed Bacon's development of the experimental method, and subsequently produced the paradigm shifting and revolutionary discoveries of Galileo and Newton, had not been adequately extended into the social, political, and moral domains of human experience.

The foundation of Comte's positivism edified the present view in education that by observing constant relations between things, including of course human beings and formulating subsequent laws or causal explanations based on these observations, the world could be understood and explained in concrete and universal terms. When considered in historical context, Comte's initial optimism is easy to understand. After all, by applying the basic principles of scientific discovery both Galileo and Newton had made tremendous strides in understanding and reshaping astronomy and physics respectively. Comte simply questioned, quite understandably given the milieu of scientific optimism prevalent in the period, why this practice, so successful in the field of natural science, was not being similarly applied to understanding all elements of human experience.

From Comte's perspective, by rejecting metaphysical and speculative explanations of human behaviour and experience, the emerging positivism held the promise of what amounted to a new religion. Indeed, it is precisely that kind of dogmatic ideological commitment outlined earlier through the views of Feyerband that drives academics in education to deny or ignore the numerous problems in the empirical research they perform. Even in its infancy, positivism revealed many of the problems – such as the confusion between normative and empirical questions – that have traditionally dogged its application to explain and predict human behaviour.

The more Comte (1974) focused on the creation of his new empirical religion – and Comte was absolutely confident if not fanatical that positivism was to become the new religion in so far as it explained the mysteries of human behaviour and experience – ironically, the further he departed from the actual positivist principles he originally supported. For example, adopting a rather troubling view espoused by Plato 2,000 years earlier, Comte committed the notorious is/ought fallacy by concluding via empirical inquiry that each person must remain in the social class most suited to his or her level of intellectual acumen. The is/ought fallacy, first identified by David Hume, mistakenly contends that because something is the case it necessarily ought to be the case. According to Comte, then, if an individual was born into a particular social class it was because they inherently belonged in that specific category.

The intellectual elite, a group Comte interpreted as the existing aristocracy who were in political control of France during this period, would be responsible for the continued administration of society because they were most capable of ensuring its effective functioning. How Comte reconciled this position with the overthrow of the monarchy during the French Revolution is unclear. In the final analysis, it seems that Comte was ultimately far more preoccupied with making prescriptive statements on the preferred direction of society than he was in adhering to the fundamental non-evaluative principles and empirical propositions of genuine scientific inquiry. But as we suggested earlier, such conflation of normative positions with empirical observations is commonplace or even ubiquitous within education research.

In his typically illustrative and insightful fashion, Kieran Egan (2002) effectively details that it was also during the nineteenth century when a British scientist and philosopher by the name of Herbert Spencer was having similar thoughts about applying scientific principles to various areas of human experience. Spencer (1928) was especially interested in determining how science could improve education during a time when schools were playing an increasingly important role in shaping British society by responding to its shifting human capital demands.

The Industrial Revolution offered many new financial opportunities to emerging entrepreneurs, but it also created the immediate educational challenge of training a labour force adequately prepared to meet growing workforce requirements. The introduction of scientism into education predictably coincides with the instrumental demands of industry, a relationship even more palpable within our contemporary schooling context. One of the implications of scientism for education is that foundational questions are typically ignored and instrumental educational aims are assumed that invariably promote the socio-economic status quo by responding to hegemonic human capital requirements.

Perhaps most infamously remembered in academic circles for asking the obviously non-scientific question, "What knowledge is of most worth?," Spencer's enduring influence on education (although his name or influence is not widely recognized) is at least partially the result of the fact that contemporary answers to this question, as reflected in present curriculum patterns, differ little from the same utilitarian responses he provided some 150 years ago. Following Plato and Comte's views on natural social stratification, his "scientific" analysis of education similarly considered disparate levels of academic achievement the natural outcome of differing intellectual abilities. Within such a framework, individuals and students are considered the authors of their own unfortunate genetically determined circumstances. Hence, the present focus on fixing the impaired student or teacher rather than addressing the social structure of opportunity is rooted in the very earliest attempts to apply scientific principles to education.

Spencer (1928) argued that the purpose of education was preparing students for the practical experiences of life rather than focusing on subjects such as classics and history that he considered a waste of valuable academic time and resources. Spencer's classification of life experiences, taught through educational aims, in order of his proposed priority included: (1) those ministering directly to survival; (2) those securing the necessities of life, contributing indirectly to self-preservation; (3) those which support the rearing and discipline of offspring; (4) those which support one's social and political relations; and (5) those which comprise leisure time, satisfying tastes and feelings (Tanner & Tanner, 1980).

Although these aims are broad and somewhat ambiguous in scope, there is a noticeable absence of emphasis on critical democratic citizenship or on any form of critical learning more generally. Instead, the entire focus is placed on the utility or instrumental application of knowledge for presupposed purposes designed to help students fit into a predetermined social context. For example, an education supporting a student's political and social relations involved accepting and acting within the class and/or social circumstances in which a learner was presently situated. As we noted earlier, Spencer viewed social stratification, as well as differences in educational outcomes, as the inevitable consequence of inherent genetic differences in intellectual ability. The role of education, in his view, was to encourage preparation for and not critical reflection about prevailing social norms.

Spencer's (1928) sweeping faith in science as a mechanism to address all possible academic and social ills is apparent in his discussion of aesthetic appreciation, an area that many radical empiricists and logical positivists including A. J. Ayer (1952) later reduced to the realm of metaphysics:

> We find, then, that even for this remaining division of human activities scientific culture is the proper preparation. We find that aesthetics in general are necessarily based upon scientific principles, and can be pursued with complete success only through an acquaintance with these principles. We find that for the criticism and due appreciation of works of art a knowledge of the constitution of things, or, in other words, a knowledge of science, is requisite. And we not only find that science is the handmaid to all forms of art and poetry, but that, rightly regarded, science is itself poetical. (Spencer, 1928, p. 58)

Spencer's account of aesthetics, a relatively slippery and subjective area certainly not subject to any standard empirical test as verificationists and logical positivists would later point out, arguably marks the genesis of scientism as a prevailing ideology in education.

More generally, Spencer's particular version of what counted as appropriate schooling lacked the critical and transformative aims consistent with the learning objectives that prepare citizens within participatory democratic societies. Instead, attention and content was focused almost exclusively on meeting instrumental aims consistent with satisfying the needs of industry and the utilitarian expectations of a predetermined social order. After 150 years of scientism in education, precious little has changed regarding this instrumental and non-critical focus of education research.

We mentioned previously that Spencer shared Comte's conclusion that different economic classes merely reflect the natural intellectual divisions of humankind where some people are more capable and therefore inherently more financially successful than others. The continued widespread belief in education that empirical research affords a solution to pedagogical problems similarly denies the reality of how many individuals are educationally marginalized on the basis of economic class or cultural context from the social, cultural, and intellectual capital that promotes academic achievement. The idea that differences in both economic and educational outcomes are a function of natural stratification is as wrong now as it was in Spencer's period and, yet, as academics in education we fail to place this issue at the forefront of dialogue with government officials and policymakers.

In his classic work *Getting it Wrong From the Beginning: Our Progressivist Inheritance from Herbert Spencer, John Dewey and Jean Piaget*, Kieran Egan (2002) marvelously illustrates that many of the flawed pseudoscientific practices pursued in contemporary education, most often under the banner of progressive education and, we would add, the more popular and contemporary ideas associated with radical constructivism, originated directly from the fallacious nineteenth-century presuppositions adopted and advanced by Herbert Spencer. Whatever we may think of Spencer's limited understanding and misguided application of science, there is no disputing the fact that he constituted a major intellectual figure in the philosophical lifeblood of the Victorian era and his impact, especially in education, as Egan accurately points out, continues to be felt in very real ways today.

Spencer's misunderstanding of science was not limited to its potential application within the field of education. For example, he was a leading proponent of the misguided Lamarckian theory of evolution, an incorrect understanding of evolution that proposed an organism proactively rather than randomly adapts genetically to its respective environment (Egan, 2002). According to this view, a giraffe has a long neck not because longer-neck mutations led to superior biological outcomes, but because giraffes had to stretch their necks to reach the limited food supply found in high trees on the plains of Africa.

In spite of his questionable scientific knowledge, Spencer's public and professional reputation during the Victorian period actually rivaled that of Charles Darwin, and he was even more popular in the USA than he was in Great Britain. Spencer was probably most recognized during the period, and later reviled by those who appropriated many of his educational ideas without crediting him such as Dewey and Piaget, for applying survival of the fittest principles, or what might be more contemporarily described as "social Darwinism," to his general investigation of both society and education. These controversial views had direct implications for his ideas about education (Egan, 2002).

As we previously noted, Spencer assumed that poor people were biologically inferior to wealthy individuals and, therefore, any attempt to improve the social and economic circumstances of the dispossessed or increase their political participation through education was a useless waste of valuable social resources. According to Spencer, this was an indisputable and presumably empirically verifiable social fact. All one had to do was evaluate the intelligence of lower class individuals to illustrate their intellectual inferiority. His proposed alternative to improve education and society involved a troubling form of genetic engineering that prevented, or at least strongly discouraged, poor people from procreating to enable society to rid itself of the scourge of human inferiority and the corresponding poverty he believed it generated (Egan, 2002).

Spencer developed a number of dubious principles for application in education that were only loosely derived from the science of his day. Indeed, sometimes in his work it is extremely difficult to separate the metaphysical claims from the empirical ones. One especially influential principle he developed that continues to affect contemporary educational design is the claim that children's learning must begin with simple ideas and progressively advance to more complex conceptions, or the view that learning inevitably moves from the simple to the complex. This widely accepted view is most notably reflected in Jean Piaget's child development theory maintaining that young children are basically inept concrete thinkers and only later acquire the cognitive capacity for more abstract and complex thought. Many curriculum developers, teacher educators, and teachers continue to hold this problematic theory as true and our entire public education system, with its K-12 structure, remains based on this idea.

Such a fundamentally misguided view of children disregards the abstractions they master during early language acquisition by understanding the multiple applications and abstractions of even the most basic concepts such as cup and chair. As an anecdotal case in point, one of us has a precocious 7-year-old daughter presently enrolled in a French immersion programme. The rapidity of her second language development is something most adults attempting a similar achievement could only dream about. Far from the inept thinker Spencer's principle of learning and Piaget's theory suggest, this young girl's progress, and her warranted impatience with her father's linguistic ineptitude, is a powerful indicator of how children's cognitive capacity actually exceeds that of adults in many areas of learning such as language acquisition.

Egan (2002) points out that the widely held education principle of moving learners from the concrete to the abstract – one obviously in need of complete revision or preferably outright rejection – actually originated with Spencer's commitment to the flawed scientific theory of Karl Ernst von Baer who suggested humans are part of an immense cosmological process shifting inexorably from the homogeneous to the heterogeneous. As part of this immense process, Spencer believed that humankind similarly begins in a concrete or simple form and moves toward increasing measures of cognitive complexity. In order to be successful, education must mimic this cosmological process. According to this view, we are transformed from our humble and rather inept intellectual beginnings as humans into eventual cognitive giants capable of sophisticated and complex thought.

Reflecting both the ability of science to impact on education and its misguided but enduring influence, Helmholtz's Second Law of Thermal Dynamics developed in the later nineteenth century, effectively terminated von Baer's cosmological paradigm, but the principle developed by Spencer based on von Baer's view continues to influence education. Helmholtz contradicted von Baer by discovering that the universe is actually moving toward increasing degrees of homogeneity rather than greater degrees of abstraction or complexity. This discovery purportedly devastated Herbert Spencer but obviously had little influence on the general commitment to stage development theory, or the idea that education must move from the concrete to the abstract as evidenced by the subsequent work of Piaget (Egan, 2002). The real enduring tragedy is that this misguided principle continues to influence contemporary educational design in a very widespread fashion. Many teachers still view children, at least in formal education, as intellectually inferior, miniature, and more primitive versions of adults who must be subjected to the "civilization" process that supposedly creates more cognitively adept adults.

Recapitulation theory also deeply influenced Spencer's developing ideas on education (Egan, 2002). Now generally dismissed as ludicrous, this theory suggested that appropriate individual development achieved through education parallels the development of Western civilization. The young and undeveloped child, then, represents a primitive being of sorts who must be transformed through education into a civilized person. Of course, a civilized person from this perspective is narrowly defined as someone who reflects the culture and mores of nineteenth-century England. Although this conspicuously Eurocentric theory influenced the subsequent developmental theories of Dewey and Piaget, it grossly underestimated the intellectual abilities of children who, as we suggested earlier, quite obviously enjoy specific cognitive advantages over their adult counterparts in areas such as language learning and imagination. Although ostensibly rejected, the theory's influence endures within contemporary education in a variety of ways, including the normative assumption that white middle-class or upper middle-class values represent the standard for appropriate conduct and beliefs.

Recapitulation theory also provided the basis for a form of eugenics and offered a convenient tool to discriminate on the basis of "science" against non-European ethnic groups in education and elsewhere. These groups were viewed as inferior to white Europeans because their particular cultural nuances and appearance failed to match those of Western civilization and European culture. African culture in particular, largely agrarian and nomadic in nature, was singled out for being exceptionally primitive with the corresponding inference that people of dark skin colour with their "ape-like" appearance, were naturally inferior to and less capable than whites.

The pervasive influence of scientism on contemporary education is in some sense, then, an enduring legacy of both Comte's and Spencer's belief that science provides the optimum method to improve human understanding, educational practice, and society more generally. As we have illustrated, it is a legacy laden with scientific error and comprises an epistemological hegemony within education from which we and our children still suffer today. It is a legacy we hope to challenge and transform in the course of our ensuing discussion. In Section 2.3 we describe the basic principles of logical positivism, the movement on which scientism is based, in anticipation of the more comprehensive critique advanced in future chapters.

2.3   The Major Principles of Positivism

In order to evaluate the merits and demerits of the dominant methodological tradition in education research, it is necessary to understand some of the basic tenets and assumptions of logical positivism, the philosophical movement founded by Auguste Comte. Shortly after World War I, a distinguished group of mathematicians, scientists, and philosophers held regular meetings in Vienna, Austria, to discuss recent developments in logic, including Ludwig Wittgenstein's (1975) *Tractatus*.

Under the leadership of Moritz Schlick, this initially informal gathering soon became known as the Vienna Circle and its members collectively argued for a systematic reduction of human knowledge to claims based on logical and scientific foundations. Logical positivism, or logical empiricism as it is sometimes called, permitted only logical tautologies and observations from experience to count as knowledge. Indeed, members of the Vienna Circle dismissed as nonsensical the metaphysical and normative claims of many long-standing philosophical traditions because they failed to meet these two fundamental criteria. The logical positivist assumptions emerging from the Vienna Circle were gradually extended into the various fields of human inquiry.

Some logical positivists argue that since the logic and processes of scientific inquiry are virtually identical regardless of the studied phenomena, no distinction is necessary between the methodological rules of natural and social science. Logical positivism focuses primarily on the observation and analysis of behaviour as if such analysis could occur in the absence of extraneous normative or contextual considerations. By adopting such an approach, it attempts to detach human behaviour from the individual or social circumstance in which it occurred. Such an analysis or understanding of human action also coincides with doctrines of empiricism in philosophy of science and the defense of behaviourism in psychological epistemology (Ricoeur, 1978, pp. 1238–1259).

The materialist, or behaviourist, understanding of human action has been criticized in a variety of ways ranging from existentialist and phenomenological interpretation (Ricoeur, 1967) to a functional theory of meaning and structuralism. In Chapter 1, we pointed out that such an understanding of human action ignores the possibility of free will and spontaneous decision-making unaffected by identifiable causal antecedents. At the core of these criticisms is either the recognition that humans possess some measure of free will or agency, or that humans are directed by normative rules and predilections that necessarily undermine strict scientific cause and effect relationships.

According to Charles Taylor (1971), human action is best understood as a narrative or story, written by behavioural characters. Thus, human action requires interpretation or analysis and explanation at the individual level in order to be properly understood rather than imposing pseudo-categories that neatly but erroneously compartmentalize human behaviour. Taylor is also appropriately critical of the empiricist ideal of verification as espoused by positivists because the position only makes sense in the context of brute data collection – i.e., data borne from natural facts whose validity cannot be questioned by offering other interpretations, or in cases where data cannot be undermined by further or alternative findings. In education, of course, alternative or competing findings are extraordinarily easy to identify in virtually any area of empirical study (McClintock, 2007).

Perhaps the major criticism against empirical interpretations of human action is that as far as the nature and analysis of an action is concerned, that action or behaviour has different meanings within different contexts. The conceptual interpretation of an action is devoid of meaning unless the intersubjective and subjective meaning of the action for the participants is taken into consideration. For example, simply stating that "Jean Valjean stole a loaf of bread. Hence, Jean Valjean is a thief" may advance an empirical claim but the statement fails to capture the complex contextual antecedents related to the circumstances precipitating the theft. Is taking the loaf of bread a theft or is it more correctly understood as a case of redistributive justice? It is one thing to give a description of an event and quite another to provide an interpretive or normative analysis of that situation. The meaning of the act cannot be captured or understood in the absence of the specific history and context, both personal and social, in which the particular event in question occurred.

When these important nuances are omitted in empirical social science research, the explanations that follow are necessarily banal and woefully incomplete. As Bernstein (1978) explains:

> Human behavior – what many linguist philosophers have called 'action' to distinguish it from 'behavior' understood as physical movement – is rule governed. The very notion of following a rule presupposes inter-subjective conventions and agreements. Rule following behavior is therefore essentially social behavior. (p. 76)

According to Taylor (1971), interpretations of human (social) behaviour produce surplus meaning that cannot be rigorously explained by brute data, and thus human action is considered outside the logic of simple verification as envisioned by the Vienna Circle, and therefore beyond the realm of scientific explanation. It is worth citing Taylor directly to elucidate this important point with obvious and direct implications for empirical research in education:

> This epistemology [verificationism] gave rise to all sorts of problems, not least of which was the perpetual threat of skepticism and solipsism inseparable from a conception of the basic data of knowledge as brute data, beyond investigation – it goes marching on, among other places, as a theory of how the human mind and human knowledge actually function. (p. 8)

Taylor further criticizes empiricism as a human research practice because it fails to appreciate context. Instead, in its most radical form, empirical research calls for interpretation of human actions in isolation and not in conjunction with social rules and conditions. In Chapter 6, this problem is discussed more fully when we underscore the error in education research, and the corresponding neo-liberal ideological advantage, by targeting students, teachers, and administrators as individuals rather than addressing the social structure of opportunity in determining educational outcomes. For example, the actual social situation of the students in standardized testing, although sometimes recorded, is not considered a primary unit of analysis in understanding outcomes. Without understanding and addressing this social context, we are left with significant distortions in any analysis of the variables affecting student learning.

In his ground-breaking essay Does Political Theory Still Exist? Isaiah Berlin (1962) addresses another crucial issue in social science. Berlin's most significant contribution was warning researchers that there are a number of important and vital questions in social science that cannot be answered by empirical methods, an aspect of empirical research we pointed out earlier in this chapter. It is precisely these philosophical or normative questions that dominate education since the discipline is by nature a conceptually contested enterprise. Berlin (1962) refers to normative questions as philosophical questions that concern matters of subjective value or personal preference. For example, he comments on the normative nature of such concepts as authority, sovereignty, and liberty by arguing the following:

> What makes such questions prima facie philosophical is that no wide agreement exists on the meaning of some of the concepts involved. There are sharp differences on what constitutes reasons for actions in these fields; on how the relevant propositions are to be established or even rendered plausible; on who or what constitutes recognized authority for deciding these questions; and there is consequently no consensus on the frontier between public criticism and subversion, or freedom and oppression and the like. (p. 7)

For Berlin (1962) human action is largely dependent on human desires and interests (non-empirical elements), and thus it is impossible to compartmentalize human behaviour via empirical analysis into categories such as subjective/objective and private/public. Berlin further argues that any attempt to objectify human action will never lead to the desired "value-neutrality" or "objectivity." In fact, these cherished tenets of LPE would themselves act as ideological biases that LPE purports to eliminate (Berlin, 1962).

Put more simply, the normative components of our actions cannot be stripped away from human experience without significantly distorting the meaning of that experience. Rather than liberating social and human sciences from biases, a dogmatic adherence to empirical methods places researchers in what Berlin (1962) describes as an epistemological "straight jacket:"

> The history of thought and culture is, as Hegel showed with great brilliance, a changing pattern of great liberating ideas which inevitably turn into suffocating straightjackets, and so stimulate their own destruction by new emancipating, and at the same time, enslaving conceptions. (p. 19)

This is precisely the case with scientism in education as we, as academics and researchers, clearly have placed ourselves in an epistemological and methodological straightjacket from which we struggle to escape in order to consider more effective approaches to the study and development of education strategies.

Michael Friedman (1999) suggests the publication of Quine's "two dogmas of empiricism" (1951) and Kuhn's *The Structure of Scientific Revolutions* (1970) marked the demise of the "philosophical movement known as logical positivism or logical empiricism" (p. 1). However, we are of the opinion that while this was indeed the point in time when major philosophical and intellectual challenges to the dominant movement emerged, the flourishing of LPE as a research methodology, as evidenced by contemporary research in education, is far from being in active retreat. Within mainstream empirical research in education, these works barely caused a blip on the radar screen.

The rumours reporting the death of LPE, as it turns out then, were greatly exaggerated. After a brief eclipse, the movement has re-emerged with renewed vigour, especially in education, and is thriving in the overall environment of neo-liberal economic and neo-conservative political ideologies that pursue instrumental learning objectives at the expense of critical reflection and moral debate. The hegemonic value of LPE as a reproductive ideology involves its protection of the status quo since discussing values, at least ostensibly, is routinely excluded from the realm of mainstream "empirical" discourse.

The dogma of scientism creates problems for researchers not only related to questions of value, but with understanding how social structure impacts on individual action and, in the case of education, on academic opportunity. Although we believe that human action is not solely determined by structural forces, any inquiry that does not take into account social rules or influences such as politics, economics, culture, and ideology inappropriately excludes from analysis these critically important forces that inevitably shape human belief and action. Bernstein (1978) describes the problem as follows:

Action is intrinsically meaningful; it is endowed with meaning by human intentionality, i.e. by consciousness. If the meaning of an action is its corresponding projected act, then it makes no sense to speak of an action without reference to its meaning. And in focusing we can and must speak of its subjective meaning, the meaning it has by virtue of the meaning-endowing intentional act of a human consciousness as well as its objective meaning – the meaning-structure that the action exhibits and that can be abstracted from it. (p. 145)

Such meaning of course lies at the heart of human action, as illustrated by our Jean Valjean example, and yet can never be captured through empirical research that reports on human action as if it were devoid of subjective purpose and meaning. To understand the meaning of an action, we must understand the individual and social context within which that action takes place.

Peter Winch (1966) argues that the idea of a social science based on the methods of natural science is a fundamental mistake because "the understanding of society is logically different from the understanding of nature" (p. 72) in that the dynamic concepts central to the understanding of social life are incompatible with those at the heart of prediction in natural science. The concepts of social experience are constructed by human agency on the basis of value and cultural preferences while the phenomena of natural science are what Taylor described earlier as "brute" concepts – i.e., phenomena that occur beyond the scope of human action.

Winch (1966) also argues that in the systematic study of social phenomena, careful attention must be paid to the rules that govern the activity of the individual participating actors and to the contextual criteria related to that action. For Winch, these rules emanate from both cultural and social institutions, and are thus dependent upon the cultural as well as the social context in which they are constructed to meet standards internal to the society or context in question. In this sense, Winch argues, logical relations between observed events or individuals involved in these events are inevitably dependent on the context of social relations.

An extreme form of such criticism can be found in the works of Feyerabend (1975) and Louis Althusser (1973). Feyerabend adopts a position he refers to as "epistemological anarchism" principally in opposition to the dominant conception of natural science in the positivist school (Feyerabend, 1975). Feyerabend's thesis appears to be constructed on non-empiricist principles, but the problems and terms of empiricism still persist within the discourse (Counihan, 1986; Denzin, 1997).

As a structuralist, Althusser contends that "the appropriation of reality is not the result of the action of the individual reason or experience, but of determinate systems of concepts" (Counihan, 1986). Althusser's (1973) position follows from the Marxist position that ideas, as part of the prevailing superstructure, are inevitably directed and controlled by what benefits the hegemony or ruling class. The former considers education merely the best available means to wrap students in ruling ideology, shaping their consciousness in such a way as to minimize any threat to the economic status quo. We will have much more to say about structuralism and its implications for education research during our discussion of Durkheim and Levy-Bruhl in Chapter 3.

A theory is defined in the LPE tradition as a set of concepts plus the interrelationships that are assumed to exist among those concepts. A theory also includes consequences or outcomes that are assumed to follow from the relationships proposed in the theory. The function of theory is to order data in a system of logically meaningful and verifiable relationships. It is further assumed that data are open to empirical observation and that facts derived from the data are neutral, objective, and unproblematic. The gap between the theory and data is bridged by means of operational definitions. There is supposedly no direct human intervention in either theory selection or in bridging theory and data. For example, an empirical test of intelligence, the IQ test, operationally defines an intelligent person as one who scores well on the test. The problem with such operational definitions, however, is that they are embedded with contestable normative assumptions, i.e., human interventions, determining the qualities that correlate with the concept in question. This moves theories and their implications in education from the domain of science into the realm of subjective and contestable normative assumptions.

In education research, operational definitions abound and are present in the empirical testing of so-called cognitive capacities such as critical and creative thinking. Since critical thinking does not connect to any objectively determined cognitive process, a good critical thinker is typically defined as someone who happens to do well on a particular critical thinking "test." Many of the so-called measurements in educational psychology, including intelligence testing and assessments of giftedness, suffer from this same confusion of conflating philosophical or normative concepts with empirical testing. The distinction between philosophical and normative questions identified as absolutely crucial by scholars such as Berlin, then, is largely ignored by a great many researchers in education.

Considerable emphasis is placed on the empiricist principle of verification as a theory in social science and verifiable data is considered the ultimate source of knowledge. Consistent with the LPE movement that emerged from the Vienna Circle, any theory or truth claim that cannot be empirically verified is thus considered unscientific. In response to this position, Feyerabend (1975) argues:

> Facts and theories are much more intimately connected than is admitted. Not only is the description of every single fact dependent on some theory, but there also exist facts which cannot be unearthed except with the help of alternatives to the theory to be tested, and which become unavailable as soon as such alternatives are excluded. (p. 39)

In a very real way, and to illustrate Feyerband's point, the idea of empirical verification as a theory of knowledge rests entirely on metaphysical assumptions since its foundational precept that only empirically verifiable statements qualify as propositions cannot itself be empirically verified, a problem with verificationism we elucidate upon later in the text.

For logical positivists, then, the hypothetico-deductive model is the ideal mode of inquiry. Theory building in accordance with this model often focuses attention on reaching a single valid explanation that in turn can explain a variety of antecedent causal factors involved in generating the observed phenomenon. In doing so, empirical generalizations hold an important if not central position, all at the expense of virtually ignoring, once again, the fundamental role of individual differences, context, and agency as central factors affecting human action.

As is the case with human action and behaviour, propositions about teaching and learning contain explanations that are inevitably context-bound and, thus, a single valid universal explanation, or the formation of axiomatic principles, is simply not possible. This basic limitation of all the social sciences, including education, renders universal claims identifying appropriate teaching methods, or claims of best practice, highly problematic as well as logically invalid. They are logically invalid because any universal claim advanced based on a limited number of observed cases necessarily falls into that logical category. For example, as a basic point of logic, one cannot claim that all ducks are black without having observed the entire class of ducks. Claims of "best practice" in education result from a very limited number of observations and, hence, all such claims are by definition logically false and highly problematic.

When exploring human experience more generally, there can and does exist any number of adequate and reasonable explanations for an observed phenomenon depending upon the social context, the observer's analytic lens, and the nature of the participants. As A. R. Louch (1966) writes in *Explanation and Human Action*:

> The nature of explanations depends upon the kinds of things investigated and on the exemplary cases we bring, often unconsciously, to our inquiries. A coherent account of explanation could not be given without attending to the audience to whom the explanation is given. (p. 233).

In general, we can conclude that theory building in social science essentially emulates theory building in the natural sciences, but introduces an entirely new set of problems related to the reporting of human experience. The influence of LPE in social science theory development necessitates that social science theories be empirically verifiable and descriptive with an accent on accuracy, internal cohesion, scope (universality), simplicity, fruitfulness (utility), and reproducible results, rather than on moral or prescriptive statements. However, as we illustrate during our examination of research in education these normative statements or positions are typically assumed tacitly in the research design.

In social science, the genealogy, to use Foucault's (1991) term, of supposedly neutral social science research can be traced back to the work of Max Weber who was inspired by the Kantian distinction between fact and value. Weber argued that the social sciences, if they were to qualify as science in any meaningful sense, must only deal with the factual side of this distinction (Bernstein, 1978).

More recent social theorists such as Robert Merton, while trying to arrive at theoretical foundations for social analysis, essentially ended up applying the same theoretical orientations used by the natural sciences to the social sciences. This emulation of natural science theory building in the social sciences left little room for human agency in theory development or in theory choice and left the social sciences labouring once again under the burden of false science (Bernstein, 1978). However, and this is the problem confronted especially by researchers in education, the mere description of human action in the absence of inferred understanding or inferred causation is tantamount to a scientific and pedagogical dead end. More directly, such acceptance of this limitation could never provide education with the universal pedagogical principles it continues to pursue since to observe a learning outcome without understanding its cause fails to identify the antecedent forces of "effective" instructional principles.

Perhaps one of the most significant attempts to break the stranglehold of LPE in social science theory building came with what is popularly referred to as the linguistic turn in social science. Original works with respect to the role of narrative interpretation of human action include those by Gadamer, Ricoeur, and Habermas. More contemporary works include those by Taylor, Winch, and Louch. In particular, Louch (1966) argues that the very idea of a science of humankind is untenable, a position as we pointed out earlier that was originally adopted by David Hume as early as the eighteenth century. Louch (1966) was especially sceptical about the emulation of natural science theory building in social science that resulted in a preoccupation with generalization, value neutrality, and verification, qualities he argued that simply do not lend themselves to the study of human beings or the analysis of human behaviour. The implications of Louch's position for developing a science of education are exceptionally obvious.

In the introduction to his ground-breaking book *Explanation and Human Action*, Louch (1966) argues that in social science ad hoc explanations have a special value:

> When we offer explanations of human behavior, we are seeing that behavior as justified by the circumstances in which it occurs [and] that what we observe depends as much on language as upon eyes, on techniques as much as on events. (p. 4)

Thus, Louch emphasizes that the natural and social sciences are fundamentally different in terms of the concepts and methods used for analysis, the consequences and predictive capacity of the advanced theory, and the intellectual heritage on which theory building occurs:

> If either the inductive or the hypothetico-deductive strategies are taken as paradigm, something must be done about putative ad hoc accounts [for] we have, in fact, a rather rich knowledge of human nature which can only be assimilated to the generality pattern of explanation by invoking artificial and ungainly hypotheses about which we are much less secure than we are about the particular cases the generalizations are invoked to guarantee. (p. 3)

Louch (1966), similar to many other social science critics we have discussed in this chapter, emphasizes the role of values and contexts in describing human action. As he appropriately explains, human action cannot be "observed, identified or isolated except through assessment and appraisal" (p. 56) and such assessment and appraisal is not sequential. In other words, the assessment does not follow from the data but precedes and ultimately shapes it – recall the claim that "Jean Valjean stole a loaf of bread." Louch (1966) describes the problem as follows: "[T]here are not two stages, an identification of properties and qualities in nature and then an assessment of them. [T]here is only one stage: The delineation and description of occurrences in value terms" (p. 56). The normative component of human action, the political or moral "why" related to an action if you will, cannot be separated from the descriptive component in any sensible or meaningful account of human action.

Peter Winch (1966), reiterating another crucial point we have raised previously, asserts there is a fundamental difference between the questions that science and philosophy can legitimately investigate. While science is occupied with investigations of the nature, causes, and effects of particular "real" things, philosophy is interested in the metaphysical nature of reality per se. In his view, questions concerning the nature of social reality are not empirical questions but essentially conceptual or metaphysical questions since society is constructed on the basis of human values unlike natural reality which is, value free. As he writes in *The Idea of a Social Science* (1966) such questions "cannot be answered by generalizations since a particular answer to the philosophical question is already implied in the acceptance of those instances as 'real'" (p. 9). Winch (1966) further argues that "many of the more important theoretical issues which have been raised in those (social science) studies belong to philosophy rather than to science and are, therefore, to be settled by a priori conceptual analyses rather than by empirical research" (p. 17). This point becomes clearer and more evident during our analysis of research into citizenship education and the idea "best practice" explored in Chapter 5.

Within education, assessing the operationally defined qualities of giftedness provides an example, where construct validity, derived from conceptual analysis, poses a serious problem. The qualities that define giftedness, similar to what counts as intelligence, are not a matter for empirical investigation since giftedness is a constructed human concept and not something that exists naturally in the world such as water, hydrogen, or gravitational force. The qualities defining giftedness in an academic context, for example, are probably inconsistent with what would qualify as giftedness among those individuals working in an agrarian community within a tropical rainforest setting, or in an urban setting where "street smarts" take priority over book learning.

As mentioned previously, logical positivism essentially rests on the assumption that facts, or meaningful statements about the world, must be observable and empirically verifiable. In other words, only those facts and theories that can be empirically verified through impartial observation qualify as scientific. Once a fact is empirically verified in this fashion, it supposedly becomes a universal fact, true regardless of context or temporal spatiality. However, what is verifiable and true in one educational context simply may not be verifiable and true in another classroom situation. We will grapple with the implications of this virtually self-evident problem for educational research at greater length in the following chapters.

The important list of personal preferences, interests, and emotions that emerge from an individual's political, economic, aesthetic, ideological beliefs, and prior cultural conditioning are disregarded and termed unscientific by LPE because they cannot be empirically verified. It is precisely these idiosyncrasies, however, that determine the very meaning of the observations in question. If these elements are not accounted for in an explanation of individual or group behaviour, the explanation remains woefully incomplete. Logical positivism contends that only empirical theories, as opposed to normative or moral beliefs, qualify as meaningful on the grounds that the former are empirically verifiable.

Values that might creep into an empirical investigation are essentially seen in LPE as biases or even as contaminants to the purity of scientific research. The dominant conception is that the research process must remain aloof from human subjectivities, beliefs, and biases, a serious problem given the predominance of operational definitions within education research. Such an expectation of objectivity is highly problematic when applied to education, then, whether the bias occurs at the level of operational definitions, the selection of the investigative context, or at the final level of analysis, interpretation and inference.

The desired rejection of value not only affects theorizing and conceptualization in social and human science but also impacts on the methodology of data collection and the methods employed for subsequent analysis. A net result of the attempted fact/value distinction in social science research is the depersonification of the research process itself. In other words, while the researcher as subject is expected to stay out of the research process (in order to act as an impartial observer) those who are studied in social science are, in turn, objectified. The interpersonal subjectivities of researchers are also often ignored or glossed over – typically in the form of confessional autobiographical statements – in the eventual claims that emerge from the research. The confession of potential bias, however, does not resolve the corresponding problem or subjective predilections that potentially shape research findings.

Values in LPE, then, although inevitably influencing research observations and outcomes, are treated as biases that supposedly have no legitimate role to play in explanation, a principle that does not and cannot hold in social science research. Generalizations (such as the axiomatic "best practice" principles sought by education research akin to immutable principles or laws in the natural sciences) become sources of empirical theorization with the potential of becoming what post-structuralist philosophers refer to as meta-theories or meta-narratives. These meta-narratives are metaphysical in the philosophical sense because their claims of universal explanation are not empirically verifiable and are, as we pointed out earlier, therefore false.

In critical theory and postmodernism, a meta-narrative (sometimes termed master or grand narrative) is a global or totalizing cultural narrative that orders and explains knowledge and experience. The prefix "meta" simply means "beyond" or "after" and is used in the context of meta-narrative to mean "about," and a narrative is simply a story. A meta-narrative, then, is essentially a story about a story, encompassing and explaining other "little stories" within totalizing schemas. The term "meta-narrative" is probably most well known for its application by Jean Francois Lyotard in the following quotation: "Simplifying to the extreme, I define postmodern as incredulity towards meta-narratives" (Lyotard, 1997, p. 56). Lyotard suggests that the postmodern condition is characterized by an increasingly widespread scepticism towards meta-narratives, such as the inevitable march of scientific progress or European civilization, as the cultural standards that are thought to provide order and meaning to Western thought. The social science narrative of LPE adopted by education researchers qualifies as a meta-narrative based on its totalizing attempt to encapsulate all knowledge about education.

Many early critics of LPE warned against the dichotomization of fact and value within social science research. For example, Louch (1966) categorically argues that such distinctions are not possible in explanatory accounts of human behaviour: "the man or situation is not [to be] seen and then appraised, or appraised and then seen in distortion; [he or she] is seen morally. Values and facts merge" (p. 54) within social science research. Much of the confusion in social science research is based on misunderstanding the distinction between social facts and natural facts, and often conflating the two categories in the interpretation of events. Natural facts describe phenomena present in the natural world beyond the scope of human decision-making while social facts are always based on acts, laws, norms, or rules involving conscious human agency and decision-making (Searle, 1995). This decision-making inevitably includes personal or cultural values regarding appropriate social organization and behaviour, and these values cannot be separated from human actions that are mistakenly described as brute empirical facts within a specific social context.

Other postpositivists such as Thomas Kuhn understand quite clearly that social facts and their interpretation are necessarily local, value laden, and context bound. It is the description of observed events and socially constructed reality in accordance with human agency or intent, along with its various contextual aspects, that determines observed outcomes. In other words, within the social sciences it is the subjects of research who construct their own reality in partnership with the values of the researcher. As Thomas Kuhn (1977) succinctly makes the point, "what the tradition views as eliminable imperfections in its rules of choice I take to be in part responses to the essential nature of science" (p. 323).

2.4   Postpositivism: A Break from Scientism?

We briefly alluded earlier in this chapter to a trend within social science research to adopt more qualitative forms of inquiry as an act of resistance to LPE assumptions. The question remains, however, what the implication of this shift entails. In this section we contend that this shift in method fails to resolve many of the previous problems we identify and, in fact, creates several new and perhaps even more serious epistemological ones.

Commenting on the neo-positivist theorists (followers of a movement characterized by alleged improvements in the manner of observation of social phenomena, through the employment of questionnaires, interviews, and other qualitative refinements of research practices) Louch (1966) writes:

> They congratulate themselves on being sophisticated enough to shun sweeping generalizations and causal observation. The apparent triviality of this research is real indeed, in the sense that our identification of social facts takes place in a way to which these precise methods have no relevance. (p. 18)

Simply changing the nature of, or tinkering with, the methodological approach does not change the nature of the problems identified through standard empirical verification. Qualitative research suffers many of the same difficulties – i.e., it remains context-bound – and confronts serious challenges concerning construct validity and generalizability. This type of research also creates additional problems such as the reliability of self-reporting and the subjective analysis of narrative as collected data. The serious problems of social science, and hence research in education, cannot be corrected by simply changing the methodological approaches. Rather, the subject matter itself rejects study that promises any significant possibility of generalizability, and without generalizability, we are compelled to challenge the purpose and/or value of conducting the research in question. Although such qualitative research may afford interesting insights into individual or group human experience, it is certainly far removed from the realm of legitimate scientific inquiry.

Following from Comte's overly sanguine confidence in human science, the positivist project aimed at making everything understandable, knowable, and predictable through the implementation of empirical methods and the procedures of rational science. Although these principles have important applicability in natural science, they have failed quite miserably to deliver the goods within the human sciences. As a movement in education, these various critiques, as Michael Apple explains in the editor's introduction to Patti Lather's *Getting Smart* (1991) "displaced, or so we hope" (p. vii) logical empiricism as the dominant research movement. Such a hope, as it turns out, was overly optimistic on Apple's and Lather's account since empirical research in education has hardly come to a decidedly screeching halt.

The disruption rather than displacement of positivism in the early 1990s created a small space for the emergence of a variety of perspectives that, for the lack of a better term, can be labeled as post-positivist research practices. Like most of the academic movements with a "post" prefix there is neither a consensus on its contours nor a precise definition of postpositivism. Within its ambit we find philosophical and methodological approaches as diverse as ethno-methodology, interpretivist, constructivist, critical ethnography, some varieties of action research, phenomenology, post-structuralism, and postmodernism.

The acceptance and application of postpositivism also varies. While some use it as a blanket category to signify the departure from positivist research and practices (Lather, 1991), others (Hammersley, 1992; Denzin, 1997) distinguish between what they term as post-positivist and postmodern. Yet still others such as Scheurich (1997) argue that postpositivist approaches remain grounded in the Enlightenment view promoted by Comte that some form of human science is possible and, hence, postpositivism is not sufficiently a turn from the fundamental tenets of positivism we enumerated earlier.

For Patti Lather (1991):

> Broadly speaking, post-positivism is characterized by methodological and epistemological refutation of positivism, much talk of paradigm shift and an increased visibility for research designs that are interactive, contextualized and humanly compelling because they invite joint participation in exploration of research issues. (p. 52)

In this sense, the common thread that runs through the postpositivist research paradigms is that knowledge (and thus research) is socially constituted and constructed, it is historically situated (contextualized) and it is inevitably value laden. These elements demand the jettisoning of a call for a science of human behaviour and the dismantling of education research as a scientific enterprise. Instead, the knowledge sought is emancipatory rather than impersonal, sanitized, and "value neutral." Postpositivism does not gloss over the contradictions in understanding, but purports to highlight them and reflects the central role of human agency and context in any observed social phenomenon. Unfortunately, of course, all of this recognition and revision is only achieved at the cost of relinquishing the axiomatic principles sought by researchers that explain learning outcomes in education in some universally applicable fashion.

Denzin (1997), on the other hand, sees postpositivism as distinct from postmodern and post-structural positions. In his view, the post-positivist position is essentially in opposition to positivism. Post-positivism calls for a new approach that is qualitative in orientation as an alternative to the quantitative orientations of the positivist research paradigm. While this approach definitely leads to a qualitative shift it "has often led to a set of criteria that are in agreement with the positivist criteria; that are merely fitted to a more naturalist research context" (Denzin, 1997, p. 8; also see Scheurich, 1997). Further, without the generalizability consistent with the positivist dream, the value of qualitative research beyond narrow versions of personal storytelling or narrative is a concern of some importance. Although this type of research may be interesting in the same way that an autobiographical or biographical story might be interesting, it entails virtually no meaningful measure of scientific value.

Other methodological problems related to postpositivist approaches, as we mentioned earlier, include the highly questionable reliability of self-reporting and the projection of researcher bias onto the research outcomes. Obviously, a move away from empirical observation and reporting intensifies risks in these areas. Ultimately, qualitative postpositive research simply introduces another set of methodological problems that raise another range of serious questions about its possible contribution to improving education. Indeed, rather than solving the problems created by positivism, we maintain that postpositivism has simply created an entirely new set of methodological concerns without adequately resolving the more long-standing ones.

In light of these issues, there is considerable debate about whether postpositivist methods even constitute a worthwhile shift from the original objectives of positivism. For example, postpositivist researchers, according to Hammersley (cited in Denzin, 1997):

> Assess a work in terms of its ability to a) generate generic and formal theory; b) be empirically grounded and scientifically credible; c) produce findings that can be generalized or transferred to other settings; d) be internally reflexive in terms of taking account of the effects of the researcher and the research strategy on the findings that have been produced. (p. 64)

Scheurich (1997) refers to such research as realist even though the claims it makes are made from positions as diverse as positivist, interpretivist, constructivist, and critical theory. This research, in Scheurich's view, assumes that it has transcended to an era of multiple paradigms but in essence it just shuffles the "paradigmatic furniture in the structure called research while largely leaving the underlying realist architecture untouched" (p. 159).

The primary scientific problems with postpositivist research are generally the same as in positivism since neither approach can possibly afford researchers the definitive axiological principles that permit the generalization of identified principles or outcomes. As such, the findings of postpositivist research are extraordinarily contextual in nature, and its scientific value exceptionally limited. This problem cannot be avoided by simply asserting that scientific outcomes are not the objective of postpositivist research practices since the fundamental value or utility of the research is necessarily thrown into question. Indeed, generalizability is achieved only at the cost of jettisoning contextual understanding and the contextualizing mantra of postpositivism is achieved only at the cost of jettisoning generalizability. Whether positivist or postpositivist in nature, social science research, and therefore research in education, is truly caught on the horns of an inescapable dilemma: claims of generalizability are unsustainable while in the absence of such claims the research value of social science, other than securing research funding and advancing academic careers, is virtually negligible.

2.5   Some Philosophical Criticisms of LPE

There are of course several other general philosophical traditions besides David Hume's radical empiricism that undermine the possibility of a legitimate human science. The existentialist commitment to absolute freedom, reflected most notably in the philosophy of J. P. Sartre, releases individuals from the behaviourist assumptions required for empirical research in education, or the social sciences more generally, to have any measure of scientific tenability, to offer a reasonable measure of predictability, or to be remotely generalizable.

For Sartre (1960), humans are condemned to be free and therefore are personally responsible for choosing their own paths and interests that are, in themselves, ethically and epistemologically immune to either predetermined direction or possible prediction. In a world where free choice rather than mechanistic causation determines human action, the idea of a human science becomes completely ludicrous since prediction at the individual level is impossible. In education, the existential classroom teacher acts as a resource to assist students in whatever project they themselves choose based on their own subjectivities, interests, and inclinations. From an existentialist perspective, this is the only "best practice" required.

To interfere with the existential experience of students is a violation of human freedom and, therefore, dehumanizing in its consequences. Within an existentialist context there is obviously little room for the generalized practices and objectives of traditionally organized education or the axiomatic principles sought through scientism. Indeed, on moral grounds alone Sartre would categorically reject the treatment of students required by positivist research practices because it objectifies human beings and, hence, interferes with their personal freedom to define themselves and pursue their personal inclinations within certain moral limits. More generally, the fundamental precepts of existentialism reject the possibility that human behaviour is either predictable or determined in the sense required by the social sciences.

The American philosophy of pragmatism, the school for which John Dewey (1916) acted as its iconic spokesperson in education, views knowledge as unavoidably contingent on context and similarly undermines the possibility of meeting the generalizability requirement of empirical research in education. According to pragmatists, what operates effectively in one classroom situation is contingent on the particular group of teachers, students, and classroom organization within that specific context (Biesta & Burbules, 2003). When the classroom variables change, the outcome of what counts as effective practice inevitably changes as well.

What we have discussed here in great brevity are only a couple of the important wider philosophical challenges to empirical research in education, but they raise a number of fundamental problems that simply cannot be ignored. If we are absolutely free as the existentialists suggest, or inevitably unpredictable as Hume proposes, then how can a definitive idea of best practice within education be identified and implemented? Context, as the pragmatists maintain, changes pedagogical variables, nuances, and outcomes, and the educational situation differs dramatically within even seemingly quite similar circumstances. Truth, according to the pragmatists, is often contingent on context, an observation from our perspective that holds exceptionally true in education classrooms in so far as identifying what works. If the context of investigation changes the research outcomes, then the idea of "best practice" in education will be dynamically connected to any contextual transformation. Ultimately, and in light of the range of problems noted in this chapter, the dream of developing a science of education seems little more than a chimera.

2.6   Current Context of Scientism and Education

Although social science generally, and educational psychology in particular, have profoundly and increasingly influenced education for more than 150 years, present statistics support Hume's initial sceptical conclusion by failing to reveal measurable gains in student academic achievement based on the scientific emphasis in educational research (Egan, 2002). In spite of this lack of significant measurable return on a tremendous human and financial resource investment, scientism and its proponents remain largely undaunted in their misguided quest for pedagogical certainty. In fact, they have been emboldened by recent government initiatives and widespread institutional and research funding support in their mission to establish empirical practice and science as the primary vehicles driving contemporary educational reforms.

In spite of the various epistemological problems and philosophical challenges we have highlighted, scientism now represents the gold standard of research methods in public funding initiatives such as the No Child Left Behind legislation and the National Research Council in the USA, and increasingly with the Social Sciences and Humanities Research Council of Canada (SSHRC). SSHRC's new funding direction is implicitly revealed in the following citation extracted from a recently released policy paper published by the Council. According to the paper, the Council's revised mission is "to generate new knowledge and understanding about the new economy and to help position Canada to better address the challenges and opportunities associated with that" (SSHRC, 2005, p. 5). Pamela Wiggins, the vice-president responsible for the Knowledge, Products and Mobilization division, suggests that:

> The agency pays attention not only to the *kind of research* [emphasis added] that is being funded but also to the *kind of knowledge* [emphasis added] that is being generated and how to systematically channel that energy into a broader society. (SSHRC, 2005, p. 5)

Of course, the "kind of knowledge generated" is expected to pursue scientific methodological practices that convey generalizable empirical knowledge and, ideally, respect the classical experimental design approach advocated by the National Research Council (NRC) in the USA. The NRC is even more explicit in its expectations by essentially refusing to fund any research in education that fails to pursue empirical methods and classical experimental design in its proposed methodology.

In a recent publication co-sponsored by the NRC (2005), Advancing Scientific Research in Education, the mantra of scientifically based research in education is conveyed as follows:

> The central idea of evidence-based education – that education policy and practice ought to be fashioned based on what is known from rigorous research – offers a compelling way to approach reform efforts. Recent federal trends reflect a growing enthusiasm for such change. Most visibly, the No Child Left Behind Act requires that "scientifically based research" drive the use of federal education funds at the state and local levels. In this context, the Center for Education of the National Research Council has undertaken a series of activities to address issues related to the quality of scientific education research. (p. vii)

In the USA, the Bush administration's No Child Left Behind (NCLB) legislation promotes scientism in education by supporting only those studies that "employ systematic, empirical methods that draw on observation and experiment" (NCLB, 2000). This same piece of federal legislation on education lacks a solitary reference to the importance of democracy or democratic citizenship in education anywhere in its pages. In Canada, the emphasis on empirical methods by federal funding agencies such as the Social Sciences and Humanities Research Council of Canada referred to earlier, coupled with the increased status of educational psychology within faculties and departments of education, offers further evidence of a growing and troubling academic confidence in the ability of empirical study, and educational psychology, to strengthen classroom practice and improve student academic achievement.

In our own Department of Education, almost the entire research and teaching emphasis outside of our own educational studies unit is placed on the promise of science and empirical research to deliver us to some kind of educational nirvana. Even within educational studies there continues at least the façade of positivist practice as the preferred template for student theses places a special emphasis on articulating the "research method" selected by the student. Our departmental doctoral programme in the pseudo-discipline of educational technology is almost entirely skewed toward statistically laden and empirically based inquiry as the only acceptable research paradigm.

As we have maintained throughout this chapter, the tangible and positive outcomes related to improving classroom practice as a result of the present focus on scientism are difficult to identify. In opposition to the prevailing contemporary academic perspective described earlier, the history of empirical research in education simply highlights an enduring and tragic failure (tragic especially with regards to the wasted human and economic resources) to improve teaching and learning in any significant or meaningful fashion.

2.7 Summary

In this chapter we have identified some of the historic and epistemological problems confronted by social science generally and science research in education more specifically. The application of scientific principles to education is marked since its inception with the conflation of fact and value, and by a range of other problematic assumptions about understanding human behaviour through empirical observation. Questions about social organization, for example, may be answered on an objective, prescriptive, and empirical level, but imperatives for social design that follow from these observations and conclusions, as demonstrated by Comte's positivism, are too often normative, hegemonic (in that they reproduce social conditions) and unscientific in nature. In education, the sweeping trend toward standardized testing provides an additional example of how values about quality learning and human action creep their way into supposedly objective measurements of student academic achievement.

In the following chapters, we continue to challenge scientism in education on various fronts including expanded questioning of the value-laden perceptions that shape research findings, the misguided but doggedly held theoretically commitments that educational researchers bring to their work, and the fact that most of what passes for empirical research in education actually draws analytic connections between ordinary language concepts. We conclude our efforts in the book by suggesting that the focus on empirical research is at least partially driven by ideological reasons and commitments designed to deflect public and academic attention from the economic and social disparity that stand at the forefront of causes related to academic failure and inequality within contemporary public education. The real problems of education are not empirical ones, but rather profoundly moral, economic, and political ones. These problems, however, involve having the very discussion that the ideology of scientism seeks to avoid by masking the problems of education as empirically solvable ones.

Chapter 3
Epistemological Problems in Social Science Research

Perspectives and Critiques

3.1 Introduction

As we have illustrated in the previous two chapters, there are a range of important challenges to empirical research in the social sciences. In this chapter, we provide additional elaboration on these critiques by exploring the epistemological problems with empirical research in the social sciences. Although the problem of pre-existing conceptual frameworks influencing research outcomes is not restricted to the social sciences, we argue in this chapter that the social sciences are more prone to widespread errors resulting from convergent thinking, i.e., thinking by researchers that remains consistent with prevailing theories and unquestioned assumptions. In the case of education these assumptions lead to errors in the dominant discourse about teaching and learning.

We also explore in some depth the positions of two noted sociologists, Emile Durkehim and Luciene Levy-Bruhl, to highlight the implications of structuralism for social science and education research. In Chapter 3, we also utilize some examples from existing educational theory to demonstrate how the epistemological issues addressed by Thomas Kuhn's idea of *scientific paradigms* and Karl Popper's *theory of falsification* are common problems in education research. We begin this chapter, then, by exploring in greater detail some of the most important epistemological criticisms of social science.

3.2 Critiques of Contemporary Social Science

For the better part of the twentieth century, inquiry within the social sciences has closely imitated the philosophical, epistemological, and methodological approaches applied in the natural sciences. Inquiry and research in education has broadly followed suit with its social science counterparts by adopting the methodological assumptions and practices applied by other social "scientists." It was not until the actual publication of Thomas Kuhn's *The Structure of Scientific Revolutions* that social scientists seriously started questioning the philosophical, epistemological, and methodological foundations of social science research.

Influential philosophers in social science such as Charles Taylor (1971) have long questioned the transposition of the assumptions and methods of natural science onto the social sciences. For Taylor, the intentionality of behaviour, or human agency, distinguishes social phenomena (human action or behaviour) from natural (physical objects) phenomena. Interestingly, Taylor and Kuhn, while in broad agreement that human and natural sciences are different and should be studied differently, disagree on how the line between the two should ultimately be drawn (Kuhn, 1998).

Since we deal with specific critiques by Thomas Kuhn and Karl Popper later in this chapter, we will only succinctly review some of the major philosophical critiques of social science in this section. As we pointed out earlier, positivism and its related movements, logical positivism and empiricism (hereafter LPE), have dominated research in social science, including educational research, for almost 200 years. During this period, but especially in the last 50 years, the movement has been critiqued from a variety of philosophical, epistemological, and disciplinary stances. The major challenges to LPE include critiques from within the natural sciences by individuals such as Kuhn, Lakatos, and Feyerabend; in phenomenology and existentialism by Schutz, Sartre, and Goffmann; structuralist critiques have been advanced by Althusser; and post-structuralism critiques were launched from Foucault and Derrida.

An important issue in the social and psychological sciences is accounting for the relationship between the observed phenomena and the antecedent causes of those phenomena. Many liberal scholars, following John Stuart Mill, argue that the natural and social sciences are linked by the possibility of an accurate prediction of events. Any differences in explanation between natural and social science are related to techniques of research and not to logic, and/or justifications by logic (Hempel, 1965, 1966; Ayer, 1959, 1975). However, while most contemporary natural science adopts the logic of *falsification* as illustrated later during our discussion of Popper, most, if not all, education research is based on the faulty logic of *verificationism*. Since we grapple with the methods of falsification and verification at some length later in this chapter, we will leave the subject for the present moment in anticipation of that discussion.

Those opposed to Mill's school of thought in social science – i.e., those who argue that the differences between social and natural science are such that accurate prediction in social science is impossible – fall under the umbrella of the Weberian tradition. Social scientists influenced by this tradition argue in favour of *comparable pluralism* in scientific methodology and the primary goal, rather than prediction, becomes that of explanation. The main assumption supporting a duality of methods, i.e., different applied methods in social and human science, is that the observer should not project the meaningfulness onto the social behaviour; in other words, the description in social science should be restricted to the behaviour itself. Scholars belonging to this tradition further argue that rules governing the meaningfulness of behaviours are not the causes of the observed phenomena. According to these critics, the motives and causes of human action can be understood by not "merely selecting those features which suit our purpose best but achieving a real dialectical synthesis of the principles involved" (Ricoeur, 1978, p. 1230).

Some advocates of logical positivism and empirical research in social science try to impress their own viewpoints on a given situation by putting forth a description in their own terms rather than the ones employed by the social agents themselves. The concern with this imposition of narrative, of course, is that these descriptions may not accurately capture the meaning of the agent's action or values. Based on this concern, critics in the social sciences distinguish between the different levels of *Verstehen* and causality, maintaining that both can be combined. *Verstehen* is broadly defined as the condition of there being present some social phenomenon while causality is the relationship between antecedent forces and the phenomenon or, in other words, scientific knowledge of the cause of the particular phenomenon in question. The problem with advancing antecedent causal inferences, even from a logical positivist perspective, is that they are non-empirical and, therefore, may reflect the values and biases of the researcher. In other instances of education research that include personal testimony, the identified causes may also reflect the narrative distortions of the research subjects themselves.

Another important point of debate involving understanding and explanation in the social sciences is the relationship between values and neutrality, and how the former influence evaluation in an inquiry into human behaviour. The questions surrounding value and neutrality are much debated in the social sciences, especially in political science and sociology, and between the positivists and the postpositivist scholars we discussed in Chapter 2. The central theme of the post-positivist school of thought is that no problem can be investigated non-politically or non-normatively, and that any depoliticization inevitably leads to mystification, or an incomplete description that fails to account for social influences.

Many of the critics belonging to the group advocating political analysis in the study of humans, similar to the structuralists we discuss in more detail later, adhere to different shades of Marxism:

> [Marxism] rejects the utilitarian, pragmatic (instrumentalist) conception of practice and the aestheticising interpretation of theory (of science, philosophy, and knowledge in general) which would seek to confer upon it a sort of existence of its own, independent of any ulterior social goal. (Ricoeur, 1978, p. 1416)

One example of this debate is the idea put forth by Habermas (1970) that technology is a value-neutral tool regardless of the context of its introduction. Alternatively, Marcuse (1964) adopts a far more Marxist analysis of technology by arguing that it is in fact a product of its historical context. He uses assembly manufacturing to illustrate this point. The assembly line was introduced into a capitalist context and its dehumanizing impact on vocational experience was embedded in its original purpose, design, and application. To understand the meaning of human experience, in Marcuse's view, one must examine the corresponding historical structural forces that influence experience. This examination occurs not in a deterministic sense, but simply in order to understand the context, intended application, and ideological implications of the technology in question.

Obviously, these various schools of thought have created considerable debate regarding appropriate methods and expectations within the social sciences. Indeed, for quite some time social scientists have been trying with limited success to attain a truly scientific identity for the social sciences (Bernstein, 1978, 1991). As we mentioned previously, this attempt to achieve scientific identity, more often than not, has amounted to an imitation of the methods and procedures of the natural sciences without the corresponding success in results.

The dominant methodological tradition of empiricism in education research operates under the assumption that the practices of natural science are wholly appropriate to investigate human phenomena. Educational researchers adhering to this school of thought borrow arguments and tools not only from natural science but also from the philosophical abstractions and logical constructions developed and presented by the positivist and empiricist schools in the philosophy of science. Broadly stated, the central argument emerging from this tradition that has deeply influenced research in education maintains any social science worth its salt must be empirically based and related claims must be subject to empirical verification. As far as scientific knowledge is concerned, then, only empirically based evidence qualifies as acceptable when it comes to answering questions about educational efficacy. For example, a representative education research methods textbook states:

> For science all evidence used for theories must come originally from the senses, it must be possible for any person who has the normal sensory equipment to be able to make the same observations. Others need to be able to replicate observations that an investigator makes. And if others cannot replicate observations under normal conditions, then serious questions must be raised about the evidence used in a study. (Selitz et al., 1976, p. 22)

This perspective maintains that every inquirer or researcher should be objective and, hence, able to make the same observations and draw the same conclusions regarding the same phenomena. On this account, the understanding of human experience is 'limited to analyzing the given theoretical content of mental products' (Remmling, 1973, p. 16).

Although the practice of impartial observation may work quite well in natural science, in social science empirical research may block our understanding of the politicization of contexts in which the collected "evidence" takes place and is shaped. A causal explanation of why humans act in certain ways inevitably involves normative and contextual components that cannot be ignored when accurately explaining individual or group behaviours. Under these conditions, claims of objectivity, reliability, and validity in human science are highly problematic. Hence, logical positivism limits the framework for research that truly captures the wide range of political and normative variables influencing human behaviour. This is especially true in studies or research that try to connect the understanding of social phenomena to political, social, moral, ideological, or complex and dynamic educational contexts.

One prevalent topic of debate in social science research involves the controversy surrounding the reducibility or irreducibility of the observed subject matter. This controversy focuses on identifying the appropriate unit of analysis within social science. On the one hand, some argue that social facts are purely social, based on the sum of human interactions and, thus, are not reducible to an analysis of individual interactions. Hence, studying individuals as subjects separated from social interaction is epistemologically inappropriate and society is therefore the proper unit of observation and analysis. The main proponents of this particular argument support the movement known as structuralism and include such famous sociologists as Emile Durkheim and Levy-Bruhl whose work we review in the following section.

3.3   Structuralism: Implications for Education

The central concern of structuralism, at least in structural functionalism, involves explaining the apparent stability and internal cohesion of societies necessary to ensure their continued existence over time. In structural functionalism societies are viewed as coherent, bounded, and fundamentally relational constructs that, in effect, function similar to organisms, with their various parts (social institutions) working together to maintain and reproduce them. The various parts of society are assumed to work in an unconscious, quasi-automatic yet orchestrated fashion to maintain overall social equilibrium. All social and cultural phenomena are there-fore considered functional in so far as they work together to achieve equilibrium and are deemed to have a "life" of their own beyond the actions of individuals. Within structuralism, individuals are significant not in and of themselves but in terms of their status, their position in patterns of social relations, and the roles or behaviours associated with their status.

The main thrust of Durkheim's (1963, 1982) structuralist doctrine is that the study of society must eschew reductionism (i.e., the study of individuals) and instead consider social phenomena as the appropriate unit of analysis. He rejects biologistic or psychologistic interpretations of human action and focuses instead on the social-structural determinants of human behaviour. To support his position, Durkheim presents a definitive critique of reductionist explanations of social behaviour. In Durkheim's view, social phenomena are "social facts" that have distinctive social characteristics and determinants not amenable to explanations on the biological or psychological level. Social facts, then, are external to any particu-lar individual predilections and endure over time while particular individuals, as mortal biological entities, die and are replaced by other individuals. It is the social facts and/or phenomena that are more constant and, hence, provide the appropriate ongoing subject matter for social science.

Social constraints, whether in the form of laws or customs, inevitably come into play, and when social expectations are violated sanctions are imposed against individuals. These sanctions are imposed on individuals to channel their various desires and propensities in socially acceptable ways. According to Durkheim (1982), a social fact can be defined as any way of acting, fixed or not, that imposes some external control over individuals. For example, a social fact in Canada is that individuals may not legally drive their cars after consuming sufficient ethyl alcohol to raise their blood alcohol percentage beyond 0.08 mg. If an individual ignores this social fact and is apprehended, a sanction is imposed. In this view, social behaviour related to the consumption of alcohol and driving motor vehicles is understood by an analysis of social sanctions rather than by analysing individual cases.

Although Durkheim's (1963) early work defines social facts by their constraining implications for action, he later focused on the operation of a given society's legal system. The mature Durkheim (1982) stressed that social facts, and more particularly the moral rules on which they are based, become effective guides and controls of conduct to the extent they are internalized by individuals. Based on this more sophisticated understanding, constraint is no longer a simple imposition of external sanctions over individual will, but rather become a moral obligation internalized by the subject to obey a rule. Post-structuralist philosopher Michel Foucault (1991) adopted a similar position to explain how human behaviour is internally regulated or policed within a society. In Foucault's view, individuals effectively police themselves by self-regulating their thoughts and behaviours to ensure alignment with prevailing social norms. Society constructs individual consciousness, then, based on internalized conformity with these dominant social expectations.

There is a historical development to social facts fundamental to understanding their role. A school classroom, for example, although composed of individual members, cannot be explained or understood in terms of its individual constitutive elements; rather, a school or classroom is a structural "whole" accounted for by the social and historical forces from which it emerges, and that shape its operation and agenda. Any social formation, although not necessarily superior to its individual parts, is fundamentally different from them and, in Durkheim's view, requires understanding and explanation on the social or structural level.

Durkheim (1982), then, was concerned with the characteristics of groups and structures rather than with the individual attributes typically targeted by educational psychology, characteristics he considered derived largely from social structure. He focused on such problems as the cohesion or lack of cohesion of specific religious groups rather than on the individual traits or personal characteristics of religious followers. He argued that group properties are independent of individual characteristics and, therefore, must be studied independently of subjectivities.

Durkheim (1994) examined different behaviours in specified populations or groups and identified the causes of anomalies such as suicide. For example, he suggested that increased suicide among a particular group indicates weakened social cohesion. Consequently, removed from social support systems, members of a group are no longer sufficiently protected against the existential crises that we, as humans, inevitably confront. Rather than seeing suicide as an individual anomaly, then, it becomes a social failing – a tenable view, but certainly not one without potential error.

Although the empirical component – increased suicide – is demonstrable, the non-empirical causal inference Durkheim advances remains open to question since suicide may also occur where strong social support is available. Hence, one weakness of studying social structure and generalizing to an entire population, a frequent failing of various forms of research in education, is that the actual antecedent causes of individual behaviours are potentially missed. Structuralism, although perhaps insightful in some ways, clearly does not afford a panacea to the generalizing problem of social science research. On the one hand, it arguably promotes the generalizations social scientists seek while; on the other hand, the generalizations may inaccurately represent the causal antecedents of individual cases.

In spite of their potential shortcomings, the positive implications of Durkheim's views for research in education underscore the importance of studying group as opposed to individual behaviour. In his view, the actions of individuals are almost entirely the result of social context. Although we sympathize with this perspective, it does not provide an adequate account of how human agency and individual choice operate outside of socially instantiated constraints and, therefore, affords an ultimately incomplete account of human behaviour. For example, we may claim that social support networks, both financial and emotional, are the primary factors in determining educational achievement and attainment, but even this claim fails to qualify as a universal principle since many exceptions are readily available. Nevertheless, the insights offered by Durkheim illustrate that focusing solely on individual action to understand human behaviour is a misguided research practice.

Levy-Bruhl examined the differences in thinking between the most "backward" societies and Western society to understand the workings of the human mind. According to Levy-Bruhl (1925), in studying mental processes and categories sociological and anthropological studies must chronologically precede (in terms of methodological importance) psychological studies because it is impossible to examine the mind prior to understanding it first and foremost as a cultural product (Cazeneuve, 1972).

The implications of Levy-Bruhl's analysis for research in education are important ones since he effectively undermines any possibility of identifying universal constructs of such concepts as intelligence since they are always derived from cultural predilections. Researchers, for example, cannot objectively define or test "intelligence" because any definition of the normative concept emerges from what is deemed consistent with a specific social context. A classic example from the field of psychology illustrates the errors when these differences are ignored in research, as well as demonstrating the tremendous damage erroneous inferences based on cultural bias can have on education.

For numerous years in the USA, it was assumed that African-Americans were intellectually inferior to Americans of Caucasian origin, an assumption often encouraged for political or ideological reasons. It is, of course, far more difficult morally to shackle another human in slavery if that person is considered socially and intellectually equal. Recall the attempts by Comte and Spencer we reviewed in Chapter 2 to explain social hierarchies on the basis of empirical research and "demonstrated" intellectual differences between classes rather than addressing the social structure of opportunity or differences in group cultural values.

Virtually all of the psychological tests employed to measure and assess intellectual, mental, and cognitive abilities (mostly IQ tests) have clearly demonstrated that Americans (mostly children and youth) of Caucasian origin score significantly higher than African-Americans of similar age (Herrstein & Murray, 1994). Higher IQ or SAT scores often set off a labeling process in schools resulting in improved access to quality education and learning experiences, and eventually improved access to more prestigious institutions of higher learning. Suffice to say, then, that such testing is not a benign and culturally neutral process of assessment.

In publishing results from cross-cultural testing, psychologists such as Herrstein and Murray (1994) disregarded the fact that these tests were designed, or "normed," for the very exclusive population of Urban, middle-class North Americans or Western Europeans of Caucasian origin. These tests include tasks (both verbal and non-verbal) and questions tested on this particular population are often not applicable to other populations that receive different schooling, employ different concepts, adopt different values and priorities, and possess different ethical mores. Moreover, the intellectual, cognitive, and mental abilities of various populations are assessed according to these tests. Hence, any significant difference in intellectual, cognitive, and mental abilities between groups should be examined to determine whether it is an artifact of the cultural bias built directly into the tests.

The most suitable method to reveal cultural bias is to devise tests that are standardized on various populations and assess the intellectual, cognitive, and mental abilities of those populations using these tests. The cognitive ability of each population is evaluated by tests standardized according to that group. This approach resolves the issue of social constructs and bias, but it does not, of course, address the more general problem of construct validity within a given culture, an issue that remains of philosophical import. However, to ensure even minimal validity, evaluating the cognitive and mental abilities of any group requires standardizing the test in question against that group. The employed concepts, values, and linguistic devices are familiar to these populations just as the standard IQ or SAT tests are familiar to the population of Urban, middle-class North Americans or Western Europeans of Caucasian descent for which they were designed.

To examine the African-American student's intellectual abilities it is necessary to acknowledge this group often constitutes a different cultural order than the Urban, middle-class North Americans or Western Europeans of Caucasian origin. These differences may often include a unique manner of speaking, thinking, and behaving. The subsequent step requires devising a set of tests that is specifically designed for African-American children and is standardized or "normed" against that population. The method of scoring could be the same as the standard tests employed on the population of Urban, middle-class North Americans or Western Europeans of Caucasian origin. Unfortunately, IQ and SAT tests are not designed with sensitivity to cultural difference in mind.

In the 1970s, numerous studies were conducted by linguists and sociologists on the dialect employed by African-Americans living in urban ghettos such as Harlem and South Bronx. The dialect, referred to as Black English, differs significantly in terms of syntax, phonology, and lexicon from Standard English (Labov, 1970), and is recognized as a unique and rich linguistic form. This difference in linguistic form led some psychologists to attribute the differences in test scores between the Americans of European ethnicity and African-American children to the latter speaking Black

English, rather than Standard English, the language of standardized tests, as their native tongue. Hence, the use of Standard English in IQ and SAT tests constitutes a handicap that impacts deleteriously on the results of the scores of the African-American children and inappropriately limits their future educational opportunities.

Quay (1971) translated IQ tests to Black English with the aid of a linguist who specialized in the language. The translated tests were administered to African-American children (a group of about a thousand children) by two African-American test administers whose knowledge of Black English and standard English was confirmed by the linguistic specialist. The original standard IQ tests were simultaneously administered to a group of Americans of Caucasian origin (of a similar size). The performance of the African-American children on their tests was found to be identical to the performance of the American children of Caucasian origin on tests normed against that population (Quay, 1971). Further, a study carried out by Genshaft and Hirt (as cited in Gross, 1987) to assess the cognitive abilities of American children of Caucasian origin using Black English found their performance extremely inferior to the performance of African-Americans of the same age and social class.

The methodology and outcomes of these studies, although important and revealing, are not really the primary concern. The issue here, as demonstrated by Quay's (1971) research, is the need to employ sociological knowledge in psychological oriented testing that determines future educational opportunities. Tests that assess the African-American students' intellectual, motivational, mental, and cognitive abilities require accommodating their cultural predilections and linguistic idiosyncrasies.

Levy-Bruhl's (1925) theory of "primitive mentality" demonstrates that differences in modes of thinking between two entirely different cultures and types of societies are unrelated to IQ assessment. He dismissed psychology, and by extension educational psychology, as too individualistic and Eurocentric in their assessments. Group influences and ethnic differences must be taken into account. Psychology explains and assesses mental processes by devising theories and tests on the basis of observing a small, specific sample and generalizing from this sample to an entire population. For example, in education, Piaget sought to explain the entire nature of human development based on a very specific sample of individuals from the same ethnic affiliation, social class, and geographic location. Levy-Bruhl's position reveals the fundamentally flawed assumptions this type of analysis inevitably entails.

In opposition to the structuralist assumptions outlined in the work of Durkheim and Levy-Bruhl, other sociologists and philosophers of science argue that inquiry must occur at the individual level since personal beliefs and intentions imbued with meaning affect social interactions and outcomes. *Methodological individualism* is founded on the assumption that when individual meaning is ignored, important differences between group members are missed and pseudo-social categories are created. In other words, individual differences are glossed over by imposing categories of description on their collective experience and action. According to proponents of methodological individualism, a serious epistemological problem arises when social situations are described in purely general or social terms, as attempted by Durkheim, without addressing the individual's social role and the correlation between individual variables and the social role played.

Structural explanations contend that what determines meaning are social structures; the individual is not the bearer of meaning, but is himself or herself determined by the meaning and/or nature of the social structure of experience. In the extreme form of structuralism, the individual as a subject with agency entirely disappears and is instead constructed psychologically on the basis of various external forces. However, such a perspective, in our view, inappropriately disregards the mediating role of human agency in shaping interactions between subjects and social structure. To discuss individuals without appreciating both the external forces acting upon them and their individual agency leaves out a critical component of identity construction. Hence, we view the division between methodological individualism and structuralism basically as a false dichotomy since both group and individual forces inevitably shape our experience. The historical context of classroom experience undoubtedly plays a role in consciousness construction, but individual agency mediates that structure in a variety of ways (Lave & Wenger, 1991; Wertsch, 1998).

When sweeping generalizations are made regarding what constitutes best practice in education complete with prescribed outcomes the individual differences students embody that affect such claims are inappropriately ignored. In other words, the ability of human agency to mediate cognitively between the structure and outcome is neglected. Although some students may flourish in a computer-based environment, others may find it antithetical to effective learning; some students may excel in literacy with phoneme instruction while others may do better within a whole language approach.

A contemporary educational psychology textbook provides an excellent example of how universal claims about best practice are sometimes advanced based on a limited number of studies while simultaneously ignoring individual differences, subjective preferences and the inevitable exceptions to the claim:

> Direct vocabulary instruction works. Probably the most straightforward research finding relative to vocabulary is that direct instruction enhances achievement. In a major review of research on vocabulary, researchers found that teaching vocabulary directly increases student comprehension of new material by 12 percentile points. (Marzano et al., 2001, p. 127)

One would not be forced to look very far in the educational psychology literature to find another study that suggests the direct instruction advocated by these researchers was ineffective in teaching vocabulary. The obvious problem, of course, is that many students in such teaching approaches become bored silly and simply tune out to the instruction. Such individual differences and propensities are simply ignored, and the veracity of related claims about best practice negatively affected.

3.4 Conceptual Frameworks Shape Research

As we have pointed out in the previous two chapters, there are various criteria for objectivity and validity that the majority of research within education simply fails to meet. To reiterate an important qualifier in our position, we are not suggesting that some of these problems do not affect science in disciplines other than education, including some research within natural science, but only that their impact is exaggerated by the multiple variables, dogmatic adherence to prevailing ideas or theories, and the human agency affecting education research outcomes.

Education is a distinctly human practice that is far less governed by demonstrable causal regularity than by surprises, disappointments, accidental encounters, contingencies, and everything else to which human circumstance and history are subjected. We have argued that education research cannot achieve the methodological objectivity of the physical sciences. To study human beings under the illusion of achieving predictive validity is to remove human experience from its personal, social, and historical context. It is to treat human agents entirely as objects of analysis rather than understand them as subjects capable of personal and social transformation.

One important measure of scientific objectivity is allowing the observed phenomena, or collected data, to inform the theoretical inferences and eventual conclusions drawn. In other words, the data must inform our conclusions rather than allowing the lens we apply to our observations to determine the research outcomes. The problem in education and the social sciences more generally is that research in the absence of some presuppositional framework or theoretical commitment is exceptionally rare and probably not even possible given the individual biases and perspectives brought to bear on any research enterprise.

A common response to this problem currently employed in post-positivist education research is simply to openly confess one's ideological bias, but this practice does not, of course, resolve the issue regarding scientific objectivity. It simply makes such bias an overt influence as opposed to a tacit one and in some cases provides a decidedly weak justification for subsequent faulty analysis. Some education research that jettisons all conceptual and personal presuppositions allegedly occurs under the umbrella of phenomenology. The objective of phenomenology is to allow the observations to stand on their own without imposing some pre-existing conceptual framework onto the data. However, even in these cases it is less than certain that presuppositions and conceptual frames are not brought to bear on the research process. As we pointed out in Chapter 2, separating human behaviour from social rules and researcher bias seems an unlikely outcome.

In other instances of educational research the influence of theory on the subsequent conclusions drawn is far more obvious. If we adopt a Marxist or critical theory analytical framework, for example, then nearly every subsequent analysis performed and conclusion drawn is the assumed consequence of underlying class-based antagonisms. Similarly, a feminist might view and explain every observed inequity between men and women as the inevitable outcome of gender inequality or male oppression. However, plausible alternative inferences or explanations are always conceivable in such cases, and these possible alternative explanations seriously undermine the scientific objectivity and predictive validity of the respective theoretical frameworks as universally valid forms of analysis.

A Marxist analysis of disparate economic incomes might ignore the different priorities and values humans hold in mapping out their individual lives. A member of the so-called working class might autonomously reject the high-pressure lifestyle associated with corporate leadership, choosing instead a life more devoted to intimate relationships with friends and family. Similarly, a vulgar feminist might ignore the cultural distinctions present in situations or cultures where women autonomously choose to live a more domestic role than men. In such cases women would rightly reject the label of oppression that some feminists might attempt to apply in defining their lived experience. In both of these cases, then, the empirical observations do not necessarily or scientifically lead to the respective causal antecedents because, as we pointed out in Chapter 2, human experience cannot be separated from the cultural context or individual agency that provides actions with meaning. The applied theoretical framework predetermines in very real ways the conclusions drawn by Marxists, feminists, psychologists, and many other social science and education researchers.

The applied observational lens, then, inevitably shapes the nature of subsequent research findings, a problem especially prevalent within education. Indeed, to employ a metaphor, it is similar to carrying around a hammer and sooner or later everything you see begins to resemble a nail. However, to stave off condemnation from Marxists, feminists and other groups holding normative theoretical commitments, we are not suggesting here, nor do we wish to imply, that there is a universal lack of validity to many of the observations advanced by Marxists or feminists. Indeed, many of their combined insights no doubt touch upon important truths concerning certain economic and social injustices within specific contexts. We are simply pointing out that researchers typically draw sweeping conclusions and make universal claims of truth based on their own assumptions rather than reporting on the actual subjectivities of those they are observing. Put another way, researchers tend to seek out, sometimes quite actively and doggedly, confirmations of their theoretical presuppositions rather than looking for anomalies that might undermine their theoretical commitments. However, these anomalies, or falsifications, are crucial components in determining the validity of a particular theory.

Instead of seeking out supporting evidence for theoretical assumptions, it is now standard practice in contemporary scientific research that researchers seek anomalies where the theory under review does not hold as true. For example, the theory of gravity would be in serious jeopardy if an object dropped from the Leaning Tower of Pisa or the Empire State Building either drifted upward or remained stationary in space. From a logical standpoint, empirical verification can never prove gravity as a universal law since there is no finite number of observed instances that can instantiate universal claims of truth. Alternatively, when anomalies are discovered, ideally, the theory is viewed as highly problematic and most probably lacking veracity, a position advanced primarily in views of Karl Popper and his theory of *falsification*. Keuth (2005) underscores the importance of falsification to scientific research by pointing out its logical foundation:

> Popper's new solution to the problem of demarcation is based on a simple logical consideration: Universal statements are not verifiable. For example, no infinite number of observations of white swans can guarantee the truth of the statement 'All swans are white,' unless the observations cover the whole population of swans, but we cannot be certain the whole population is covered unless we define it as spatiotemporally limited. On the other hand, every universal statement is falsifiable if we can presuppose the truth of at least one falsifying basic statement. If, for example, the singular

statement 'Antony is a black swan' is true, then for logical reasons the universal statement 'All swans are white' must be false. (p. 31)

In educational theories, however, such anomalies are often simply disregarded and the researchers offer some non-empirical *ad hoc* explanation to explain away the problem. When an exception to Piaget's stage theory is noted, for example, it is simply explained away by *ad hoc* claims rather than falsifying the entire theory. If some students learn more working by themselves than collaborating in groups, researchers continue to extol the value of collaborative learning as a universal truth, or best practice, by explaining away the anomaly.

In his ground-breaking text, *The Structure of Scientific Revolutions*, Kuhn (1970) suggests even natural science rarely operates in an entirely objective fashion. This problem is dramatically amplified within the social sciences since the tests of truth are by their nature far more complex given the dynamics of human agency and behaviour. The distinction between natural science and educational psychology is that flawed theories are eventually replaced in natural science. In education, the unfortunate tendency is to reshape or repackage fundamentally flawed theories in new terminology, or even defend and perpetuate them as legitimate in spite of the plethora of evidence to the contrary (Egan, 2002).

Kuhn (1970) argues that a particular paradigmatic view in natural science is held until numerous *ad hoc* principles added by the theory's proponents can no longer save it from total collapse, and then a new scientific model or paradigm is adopted by the field:

> In the course of any spell of normal science anomalies accumulate, problems and difficulties which only arise because of the attempt to fit nature into the pattern defined by the existing orthodoxy. When the extent of the anomaly gives rise to widespread unease and dissatisfaction with the existing framework of research, a period of crisis begins in which work becomes more speculative and loosely structured. Eventually practice rearranges itself around new procedures and new concepts which are thought to deal more adequately with the anomalies of the old scheme of things: a scientific revolution occurs, and creates a new basis for a sequence of normal science. (p. 11)

We will elaborate on the positions of both Popper and Kuhn as two key figures in the philosophy of science whose work highlights some of the most serious problems in education research in the following sections.

3.5 Kuhn's Scientific Paradigms

In his seminal text, *The Structure of Scientific Revolutions*, Thomas Kuhn (1970) argues that much of the progress within science often involves what he describes as paradigm shifts "in which a scientific community abandons one time-honored way of regarding the world and of pursuing science in favor of some other usually incompatible approach to its discipline" (p. 140). Although Kuhn believes these revolutionary, or paradigm, shifts are relatively rare, when they do occur they dramatically change the face of science in that area of scientific inquiry. Copernicanism,

Darwinism, and Einsteinism provide classic examples of instances where a complete or partial shift in a scientific perspective occurred.

Copernicus, for example, overthrew the idea of a geocentric universe with his discovery that the Sun was actually at the centre of the solar system rather than the Earth as previously thought by the ancient astronomer Ptolemy. Darwin seriously undermined the theological and creationist argument on human development with his theory of natural selection. Einstein demonstrated that Newton's long-standing theory of gravity failed to hold when objects travel at the speed of light. All of these cases demonstrate that science, even the natural variety, undergoes relatively dramatic shifts in theoretical frameworks and principles.

Kuhn (1970) builds on the idea that participants across disciplinary matrices understand the world differently by highlighting that their worlds are, in fact, significantly varied because of the presuppositions and assumptions they hold:

> In a sense I am unable to explicate further, the proponents of competing paradigms practice their trades in different worlds. One contains constrained bodies that fall slowly, the other pendulums that repeat their motions again and again. In one, solutions are compounds, in the other mixtures. One is embedded in a flat, the other in a curved, matrix of space. Practicing in different worlds, the two groups of scientists see different things when they look from the same point in the same direction. (p. 150)

These remarks seem to suggest that Kuhn was a radical constructivist, believing that knowledge is entirely derived from the perspective of the individual, because he implies the way the natural world is known or understood depends on prevailing assumptions and the corresponding perspective of the observer. Radical constructivism entails some form of epistemological relativism, but the latter is a position Kuhn vehemently rejects. In fact, he denied any constructivist implications resulted from his observations on changing scientific paradigms and fully accepted the possibility, even probability, of scientific progress (Keuth, 2005).

The closest Kuhn came to radical constructivism as an epistemology was to acknowledge a rather loose parallel between his views and those of Kantian idealism. In *The Critique of Pure Reason*, Kant (1934) observed that humans are incapable of knowing the *thing-in-itself*. Instead, we are collectively imbued with a shared conceptual framework that invariably shapes our perceptions and understanding of the world. Concepts such as time and space, then, are not something in the world revealed through objective scientific inquiry, but rather are more correctly viewed as part of the human lens through which we make sense of the world around us. This particular understanding of human perception puts limits on claims about absolute reality, but still permits claims of limited truth by describing how we, as humans, experience that reality.

Kuhn draws a distinction between the world-in-itself and the "world" of our perceptual and related experiences, or what Kant described as the phenomenal world. This distinction closely corresponds to the Kantian distinction between the noumenal realm and the phenomenal realm where the former includes certain conceptual presuppositions such as time, space, God, and morality, all of which Kant argues are necessary conditions of human experience. These noumena have no empirical relationship to the world-in-itself other than that they are inevitable components of human perception, experience, and understanding. Put more simply, they are the irremovable goggles through which humans experience and explain the world.

The important difference between Kant and Kuhn is that the latter regards the general form of the phenomena not to be fixed but instead changeable based on the particular science, or theoretical commitments, of a given historical epoch. A paradigm shift can lead via the theory-dependence nature of observation to a difference in one's experiences of things and thus to a change in one's interpretation of the phenomenal world. Kuhn (1970) likens the change in the phenomenal world invoked by theoretical commitments to the Gestalt-switch that occurs when we observe the duck–rabbit diagram first as a duck and then as a rabbit. He qualifies this example by acknowledging his uncertainty whether the Gestalt case is an accurate analogy or whether it merely illustrates some more general truth about the way the mind works that encompasses an aspect of scientific paradigms. Regardless, the well-known diagram does illustrate that two individuals, or even the same individual at different temporal periods, can easily see at least two different "realities" within the same observed phenomenon.

In addition to the problem of different perceptions or analyses of the same phenomena, most of the research that takes place in science, according to Kuhn (1970), involves what he describes as convergent thinking. Again, although this problem is present throughout science, we reiterate that the problem of convergent thinking in education is magnified considerably because of the persistence of flawed theoretical commitments adopted by researchers. In convergent thinking there is broad acceptance of an existing theory and the subsequent fitting of one's findings into that particular paradigm, or as he puts it, "We have attempted to teach students how to arrive at 'correct' answers that our civilization has taught us as correct" (Kuhn, 1970, p. 141). Kuhn himself actually singles out the social sciences in particular for actively discouraging divergent thinking, an observation that is especially salient to research within education, and within educational psychology in particular.

The various textbooks available within a particular science typically support existing theoretical assumptions and discourses about education often in an entirely, or at least largely, uncritical fashion. Let us assume, for example, textbooks in educational psychology simply detail the kinds of questions and conclusions that tend to support the existing paradigmatic assumptions related to such theories as stage development learning and/or to concepts such as "gifted learners" and "critical thinking." An educational psychology textbook exploring the subject of developmental learning may cite a number of experiments or names of researchers that generally confirm Piaget's notion of stage development. Any serious critical discussions of the various arguments challenging the theory, such as advanced by Egan (2002), are ignored.

Many of these same educational psychology textbooks will cite Lawrence Kohlberg's problematic theory of stage-dependent moral development as the accepted paradigm for contemporary thinking about moral reasoning. Yet, this theory has fallen badly out of favour among many noted moral philosophers such as

Nel Noddings and Jane Roland Martin who offer more sophisticated and complex explanations about the fluid decision-making processes involved in human moral reasoning.

The myriad of experiments and arguments against Piaget's theory, then, are typically ignored even in the most recent educational psychology texts. Many undergraduate students in our own foundations classes are amazed to learn that Piaget's theory is viewed as seriously flawed by many philosophers of education and even among those child education researchers who have objectively and empirically falsified its claims. Their astonishment arises from the fact that standard psychology textbooks used by their instructors in undergraduate teacher education courses treat Piaget's work as largely unproblematic (see, e.g. Woolfolk et al., 2005). Hence, new textbooks are written, new lessons taught and new theory proponents created in the complete absence of any genuine critical reflection on, or challenge to, the material.

There are various examples in education that illustrate how problematic ideas remain instantiated in formal policy and curricular development. One bit of anecdotal evidence recently presented itself when a well-respected colleague from Simon Fraser University in British Columbia, Canada, contacted one of us, seeking resources that challenge Bloom's taxonomy, a classification of human capacities that creates an untenable dichotomy between reason and emotion. This colleague reported that a recent British Columbia provincial curricular document cited Bloom's taxonomy as the theoretical foundation buttressing its design. As this colleague recognized, Bloom's taxonomy is highly problematic, and in fact warrants dismissal in our view, because it fails to recognize that emotions are derivative of reason and reason is inevitable influenced by emotion. They are not separate or distinct categories but invariably interconnected ones. To separate reason from emotion, then, is to misunderstand human cognition and emotion, and to create a false taxonomy that potentially impacts negatively on human learning. This anecdote simply underscores our contention that old and misguided ideas in educational theory typically die a protracted death if they are not condemned to a troubling sort of theoretical immortality.

There are a number of practical reasons why scientists, both of the natural and social variety, are reluctant to jettison a potentially problematic theory. These include the collegial and institutional pressure to accept an existing theory, the politics of research where some fields of study and ideas are more likely to receive funding than others, and the problem that investigating a theory's anomalies may divert a "successful" research agenda from completion. How many educational psychologists, after an entire career working in the field, are prepared to accept that their work is fundamentally flawed?

There is considerable professional, institutional, and financial pressure, then, brought to bear on education researchers to work within existing conceptual frameworks. Hence, as Kuhn (1970) suggests, it is far easier simply to dismiss the inconsistencies as instances that require further explanation within the confines of the existing theory than it is to suggest the theory itself is entirely misguided. Kuhn (1970) explains:

> Reports of effective research repeatedly imply that all but the most striking and central discrepancies could be taken care of by the existing theory if only there were time to take them on. The men [and women] who make these reports find most discrepancies trivial or uninteresting, an evaluation that they can ordinarily base only upon their faith in the current theory. Without that faith their work would be wasteful of time and talent. (p. 165)

In educational psychology in particular researchers go to extraordinary lengths trying to rescue their concepts and theories from attack. These theories, including Piaget's, continue to dominate the most influential educational psychology textbooks (Woolfolk et al., 2005), often with many of the most trenchant criticisms against the positions, as we pointed out earlier, simply ignored.

In spite of numerous discrepancies, the proponents of these theories boldly soldier on as if the purported truth they espouse was immutably captured in their textual observations and claims. The information is therefore conveyed to future researchers in a manner that perpetuates flawed belief systems to an entirely new generation of potential researchers. Barnes (1982) nicely summarizes Kuhn's observations regarding the impact of this type of indoctrinatory training, under the guise of education, and how it influences future researchers about to enter a field of academic study:

> According to Kuhn, if one looks at the extended training which precedes research in a developed scientific field, then its most evident distinctive feature is the extent to which it relies upon textbooks: the accepted terminology of a field, its methods, its findings, and its favoured modes of perception, are all conveyed through their use. And the credibility of all of these components of scientific culture depends not upon the indications of experience lying behind the exposition of the text, but upon the authority of the teacher, and the institutional apparatus which supports it. (p. 16)

In Section 3.6, we explore in detail the views of Karl Popper as elucidated in his theory of falsification and examine the position's implications for research in education.

3.6   Popper and the Concept of Falsification

The limited theory testing that occurs in education is sharply circumscribed because concepts related to a theory are typically employed to explain any observed anomalies. For example, the proponents of Piaget's theory describe students who do not fit neatly or consistently into any developmental stage as simply being between stages (Egan, 2002). Although this significantly undermines the credibility of the theory since there is no allowance made by Piaget for between stage statuses of children, the theory is rescued from complete disrepute by *ad hoc* explanations. As a result of these *ad hoc* explanations, that in theory could be added *ad infinitum*, there is little hope that a significant aggregate body of empirical data contradicting the theory will be interpreted in a manner to disprove stage development learning.

Even in the face of considerable evidence against the theory, then, its assumptions remain instantiated within teacher education, thereby influencing the level of academic challenges students confront. Egan (2002) convincingly argues, for example, that the continued application of stage development theory leads to a gross underestimation of children's intellectual abilities. The lower the expectations placed on students, the lower the levels of subsequent academic achievement. The contradictory evidence identifying anomalies in Piaget's theory is interpreted through a lens seeking to confirm rather than falsify the tested theoretical framework. As Kuhn points out, the institutional, textual, and research pressures are significant enough to insulate the theory from serious academic scrutiny.

We repeatedly return to Piaget's stage development theory, and the entire idea of developmentally appropriate learning, because it offers a paradigmatic archetype lucidly illustrating the inability of educational research to jettison problematic theories in spite of their widespread falsification. Piaget's theory also highlights the errors in using verification as a means of achieving scientific credibility since the theory's proponents are able to provide many instances where Piaget's projections actually appear true. Indeed, the conceptual machinery and *ad hoc* explanations brought to the defense of Piagetian analyses of children's learning insulates the theory from a truly scientific critique, i.e., falsification, that render it undeniably problematic. As we pointed out earlier, verification of individual and limited instances can never provide proof of a theory's scientific validity.

Egan (2002) draws attention to this problem by pointing out how Piaget's proponents seek out confirmations and supply additional explanations to protect stage development theory from the complete destruction it deserves: "Piaget's theory over the decades has amassed a considerable baggage of *ad hoc* metatheoretical glosses, whose combined contribution is to remove much of the theory from the realm of the testable. If discrepant data can be explained away, we are left to wonder what could count as evidence against the theory" (p. 33). The available criticisms of Piaget's theory are numerous, compelling and scientifically damning. These criticisms include the misunderstanding of instructional language by children (if the instructional language is changed children are able to successfully complete the task in question), observations that suggest instruction in the supposed stage-specific task changes the outcome and, as we mention earlier, many children simply do not fit consistently into any of Piaget's categories. Yet in spite of these various anomalies, or falsifications, the theory and its proponents persevere as if completely oblivious to the experimental data undermining the theory's credibility.

When considered collectively, these problems ought to cast serious dispersions on the theory's scientific status. Indeed, even a single instance where the theory does not hold ought to provide sufficient grounds to cast considerable doubt on its theoretical foundations. Unfortunately, rather than providing the impetus to jettison the problematic theoretical assumptions attached to stage development theory, they are, as Egan (2002) points out, explained away by Piaget's followers to protect the basic precepts of the theory, a predictable tendency given the various vested interests that rely on maintaining a theory's tenability.

The general scientific problem here is that in spite of numerous empirical objections against Piaget's hypothesis (instances where the theory clearly does not hold), it appears that no irrefutable contradictory evidence can be mounted to disprove stage development learning, a situation that should result in the collapse of the theory according to Popper's idea of falsification. Falsification is the theory that separates actual science from pseudoscience.

Popper is often described as a positivist since his views followed the development of *verificationism*, an attempt by the positivist movement, as we previously pointed out, to distinguish between the kinds of statements that were meaningful and those that are meaningless, but it is a label he rejected (Corvi, 1996). The essence of positivism, a philosophical school borne from the philosophers of the Vienna Circle was the elimination of metaphysics from philosophical discourse. The test of meaningfulness for verificationists was whether a statement, at least in theory, could be empirically verified. Hence, the claim that "the moon is made of blue cheese" is a meaningful statement while the claims that "God exists" or "stealing is wrong" are not. The former statement's (the moon is made of blue cheese) truth or falsehood can be empirically determined, at least in theory, while the latter statements lend themselves to no similar test. Ultimately, then, all claims emerging from ethics, aesthetics, and religion are reduced by verificationism to either mere emotive reactions or nonsensical statements.

In *Language, Truth and Logic*, A. J. Ayer (1952) adopted the major tenets of verificationism as a strategy for eliminating all religious, moral, and aesthetic statements from the realm of meaningful propositions. However, Popper (2002) dismissed this radical application of empiricism on the grounds that no unmediated theory-free statements about the world are possible or, in other words, some conjecture always precedes observation. In his view, no scientific stance, including the notion of empirical verification, was possible based entirely on observation alone. The verificationists discovered this problem themselves when they eventually realized that the *verification principle*, i.e., the claim that only empirically verifiable statements are meaningful, is not itself empirically verifiable!

Popper does not deny the importance of empirical experience to science but considered it inextricably connected to our pre-existing assumptions about the world (Gorton, 2006). His rejection of *verficationism* is perhaps his most notable contribution to the philosophy of science. In place of verificationism, Popper (2002) argued that theories, hypotheses, and conjectures, or for our own immediate purposes educational theories, can never be proved universally true regardless of the number of times they are corroborated by empirical evidence. Again, this is not an entirely original assertion since the position is directly connected to Hume's observations on induction that understood claims such as "gravitational law is universally true" were by their very nature logically false.

We might assume with good reason that objects will fall in the same pattern tomorrow as they did today, but there is no logically necessary reason why that inference is universally true. As we noted previously in this chapter, there is no logical contradiction in maintaining that objects will not fall to earth when dropped from the Empire State Building. Neither is there the possibility of observing all dropped objects. Hence, gravity stated as a universal law, is by definition logically false. Instead, based on past experience, we merely anticipate that objects will fall toward the ground. As Popper explains, "rationally, or logically, no amount of observed instances can have the slightest bearing on unobserved instances" (as cited in Gorton, 2006, p. 126). Hence, it was obvious to Popper that a superior mode of proof beyond verificationism was required to distinguish scientific claims from potentially problematic or questionable ones.

Popper (2002) believes it is notoriously simple in science to obtain confirmations, or verifications, for virtually every theory when researchers seek such confirmations. For example, if we want to find instances where Piaget's theory holds true, or cases where collaborative learning seemingly promotes the superior acquisition of knowledge, we will, almost inevitably, find such cases. But clearly such verification does not make a theory universally true or scientific. This understanding, in conjunction with the issues raised by Kuhn, partially explains the enduring credibility of otherwise highly problematic theories within education such as Piaget's theory of stage development. A meaningful scientific theory is not illustrated by confirmation or empirical verification, but rather by prohibition that forbids certain things to happen contrary to the theory's postulates.

According to Popper, the more a particular theory forbids, then the more scientific the theory. On the contrary, a theory such as Piaget's, which forbids virtually nothing, is demonstrably non-scientific. Popper also maintains, and this view widely determines the value of a theory among members of the contemporary scientific community, that theoretical irrefutability is not a virtue of a theory but rather a damning condemnation of its scientific worth. If a postulate such as "God created the universe" cannot be falsified at least in theory, then it is in fact no theory at all. Obviously, many claims emerging from education are based on verification, since they do not include observation of universal populations and are invariably falsified at least in some cases. This, of course, renders such postulates about learning as little more than misguided and logically false generalizations, and necessarily removes them from the domain of legitimate science.

As we noted earlier, Popper understands that some genuinely testable theories, when found to be false via falsification, are often upheld by their admirers through introducing *ad hoc* assumptions or by reinterpreting the theory in such a way that it escapes refutation, but this practice comes with a significant cost. Such *ad hoc* assumptions are always possible, but they rescue the theory in question from refutation only at the price of destroying its scientific status and credibility.

We contend that the implications of falsification for research in education are both readily apparent and extremely damning since even a single instance where a theory or claim does not hold affords sufficient grounds for deeming the theory in question unscientific. We are compelled, with tongue in cheek, to ask our empirically research-driven colleagues whether there are any theories of learning that lack such specific exceptions. If there are none, then how are these anomalies explained away and at what cost to the credibility of the theory in question?

Unlike verificationism, Popper's theory of falsification is based entirely on logical form rather than on metaphysical assumptions about empirical reliability. Ironically, verficationism, as we pointed out earlier, is ultimately a metaphysical position because its principles are not themselves empirically verifiable. The falsifying mode of inference referred to here, or the manner in which the falsification of a conclusion entails the falsification of the system from which it is derived, is the standard *modus tollens* formula of classical elementary formal logic.

When *modus tollens* is applied to any scientific claim or system, it may be logically symbolized as follows: Let p be the conclusion of a system t of statements that consists of theories and initial conditions (for the sake of simplicity we will not identify a particular theory but instead approach the issue as a more general logical abstraction). We may then symbolize the relation of derivability (analytical implication) of p from t as $(t > p)$ or, in other words, the claim p follows from t or "t implies p." Assume p to be false, which is written in logical terms as "~p," read as "not-p." Given the relation of deducibility, "$t > p$," and the finding of ~p, we can then infer ~t (read not-t); we regard t as falsified through a simple rule of formal logic referred to *modus tollens*. This simple formula, then, based on a basic rule of formal logic, provides the entire foundation for Popper's theory of falsification.

Alternatively, the verificationism practiced in educational research commits the notorious logical fallacy of *affirming the consequent* where $(t > p)$ results in the empirical confirmation of "p" and the subsequent conclusion of "therefore t." Translated into narrative form, then, the formula correlates with the following example: If collaborative learning is successful "t," then Johnny will learn more. The observation "p" reveals that Johnny learns more and, hence, the fallacious conclusion is drawn that collaborative learning is a principle of "best practice." Of course, the logical problem in such cases is that there could be a multitude of other conditions that cause Johnny to learn more such as his personal mood, his interest in the subject matter, or perhaps he simply gained a good night's sleep. Hence, affirming the consequent is a classical logical error and yet most of what occurs in educational research adopts precisely this invalid logical formula. As we illustrated above, Popper's theory of falsification avoids this shortcoming since his mode of inference falsifies the entire system (the theory as well as the initial conditions) that was required for the deduction of the statement p, i.e., of the falsified statement.

Our general point here is twofold: (1) so-called scientific theories in education such as Piaget's are marked by conceptual and theoretical commitments, and supplemented by *ad hoc* principles, that remove these theories from *falsification* and, hence, from the domain of actual science; and (2) there are many instances where theories such as Piaget's do not hold, or where they are falsified in practice, but they remain prevalent in contemporary educational thought instead of being deemed highly problematic or jettisoned entirely. This is largely the result of verifying instances where the theory holds true instead of focusing on numerous cases where the theory is falsified.

The unfortunate consequence, in the case of Piaget's theory and other assumptions about teaching and learning, is that the discourse of developmentally appropriate learning and other problematic pedagogical views continue to permeate curricular documents and textbooks with the attending assumption that student failure is the result of developmentally inappropriate or incompetent instruction. Once again, teachers and schools provide a convenient scapegoat for student academic failure rather than attending to the social, cultural, and economic causes that lie at the root of academic underachievement.

3.7 Summary

In this chapter we have identified a number of problems with educational research that undermine its ability to provide objective and scientific conclusions to the investigations it pursues. The problems cited with both structuralism and methodological individualism suggests neither approach fully captures the dynamic complexity of human interaction. As teachers and learners, we are both agents and objects who influence and are influenced by the context and outcomes of our social, economic, and cultural circumstances.

As Kuhn points out in his theory of scientific paradigms, the institutional and research commitment to existing research practices and agendas affords a powerful incentive to protect existing theories from condemning critiques that interrupt the production of multiple edition textbooks, threaten research grants, and undermine academic careers. These pressures combine to train or indoctrinate the next generation of researchers in education to accept passively the tenets of a prevailing theory rather than to question or reject them.

The theory of falsification developed by Popper represents the gold standard of truly scientific research and reduces all universal claims regarding "best practice" emerging from educational research as both non-scientific and logically invalid. In Chapter 4, we will present further evidence to demonstrate that most of what is termed scientific in education research related to pedagogical recommendations is actually little more than questionable speculation. In spite of the billions of dollars spent on empirical research in education, there has been heretofore incredibly little return on this investment: "The transformation that science has been consistently on the point of delivering [in education] still doesn't loom very large today" (Egan, 2002, p. 153). Why, then, in light of the paucity of success enjoyed by empirical research in education does the Bush administration in the USA, through NCLB, and the Social Science and Humanities Research Council in Canada, through standard grant applications, seek to ensure that scientific investigation remains the prevailing research instrument within public education?

Chapter 4
Empirical Research in Education

Assumptions and Problems

4.1   Introduction

In the previous chapters we have reviewed the history of social science research and introduced some of the basic principles on which empirical research, or LPE, in education is based. In this chapter we turn our attention toward identifying how the principles of logical positivism, when applied to education research, are ineffective for strengthening the discipline.

In the following sections, we address some of the most problematic assumptions involved in carrying out empirical research in education and grapple with several related problems. Some of the major assumptions in social science research that promote positivistic or scientific principles in educational research include the following claims that we deconstruct within the course of our discussion:

- Educational researchers, like physical scientists, are detached from their objects of study in that their personal preferences and biases are excluded from their subject matter, observations, and attending analyses.
- Investigations of educational phenomena can be conducted in a value-neutral fashion, with the researcher eliminating all personal bias and preconceptions and employing language that expresses objectivity. In other words, there is objectivity and conceptual clarity in describing the studied phenomena within genuine scientific inquiry.
- Educational research, like the physical sciences is *nomothetic* – that is, it is possible to extrapolate from educational research data laws that apply generally across numerous classroom and schooling contexts. In education, this assumption is particularly crucial since the search for the holy grail of some universal, but of course entirely illusive, instructional design drives much of the empirical investigation within the field. Two researchers working in different contexts who employ the same experimental method ought to arrive at the same conclusion. As we demonstrate in this chapter, within education this outcome is simply not the case.

We will demonstrate that each of these scientific principles, or assumptions, is fundamentally flawed when applied to educational research. Hence, education research is once again unable to meet the minimal standards of meaningful scientific inquiry.

Later in this chapter we will also discuss the conceptual confusions that impact negatively on education. Finally, we examine how an implicit commitment to the direct reference theory of language, and the related search for conceptual certainty, leads to ontological errors about certain education concepts and how these errors affect student academic experience.

4.2 Quality Education and Assessment Practices

In spite of the scientism that pervades research within the field, education is obviously not a hard science in the same sense as physics, biology, or medicine (Egan, 2002). As many of the social science critics we cited in Chapters 2 and 3 argue, there are profound differences between studying natural science and studying human action and experience. Although seemingly self-evident, it is crucial to appreciate this important and unavoidable difference to understand the general ineffectiveness of empirical study in education research.

Egan (2002) articulates this distinction particularly well by pointing out that education is fundamentally different from the hard sciences such as engineering and medicine in that education is unavoidably value-saturated. He argues that medicine, as a professional practice, affords a relatively clear aim for the physician in that the imperative is to improve the health of the patient or, at the very least, to ease human suffering. However, within the discipline of education, both ends and means are vigorously contested with different stakeholders often pursuing radically distinct educational aims and purposes. Of all the professional social science disciplines, education is certainly the most controversial with aims, objectives, and methods a constant source of debate between stakeholders with different political agendas and disparate normative aims.

The question of what constitutes a quality education understandably solicits a wide range of responses based on certain political preferences, assumptions, and objectives that are always contestable because they are normative assertions. A normative claim is simply an assertion based on a position of value or preference rather than one founded on an empirical proposition that reports some static fact about the world. For example, we cannot argue that Herbert Spencer was objectively "incorrect" to identify his various utilitarian ends as educational objectives, but we can point out the implications of those objectives for democratic education and other more critical forms of learning. We can also argue that other objectives ought to hold priority over those Spencer identified even though our claims are not empirically verifiable or objective. Ultimately, there is precious little about teaching, learning, and education more generally that can be reduced to simple empirical questions or related propositional claims since the entire educational enterprise is intertwined with numerous normative issues, contestable concepts, subjective preferences, and political agendas. For example, the determination of whether student x or y is receiving a quality education is primarily a function of what we mean by "quality" rather than a function of some readily available empirical assessment.

Questions about what determines educational excellence and what qualifies as excellent teaching, then, cannot be legitimately or definitively answered through empirical means. Claims emerging from the assessment of either category will always be logically limited to claims of subjective or collective preference, albeit one hopes with some attending argument suitable to support the agenda or practice in question. Of course, education is inundated with values because even seemingly benign subject areas such as literacy and mathematics are not devoid of political preferences and messages. The readings selected for students and/or the problems they are asked to solve both convey powerful messages about what is socially, politically, and culturally important. We might determine empirically what certain students do in certain situations at time t^1, then, but we simply cannot "measure" empirically whether those actions are reflective of "quality" education or learning in any objective or definitive fashion.

Critical theory, although it includes many different strands and assumptions, finds its primary source in Marxist philosophy with the fundamental idea that capitalism creates an unavoidable division between classes that leads to unacceptable levels of social disparity. When applied to education, Marxist theory suggests that schools are designed simply to reproduce these class divisions through various employed mechanisms. These reproductive mechanisms include schooling elements such as formal and informal streaming, the provision of differing credentials such as those acquired from Ivy League universities versus states ones, and a range of implied ideological messages conveyed to students through the formal, informal, and null curriculum, and through many other schooling mechanisms. The null curriculum is simply the subject matter or knowledge not included in the formal curriculum. When certain knowledge or perspectives are excluded from the formal curriculum students may assume that the information is unimportant and it is therefore marginalized from mainstream discourse.

The realization of the normative nature of quality learning (or educational quality: the two terms are used interchangeably in the literature) is increasingly evident in the redefinition of education objectives both by intergovernmental organizations such as the UNESCO and UNICEF, and within academia itself. While on the one hand there is a strong advocacy for adopting a subject-centred approach to education and defining the quality of education from this perspective, the dominant perspective is still mired in behaviourism, the epitome of positivist theorization within education. Although there are a number of perspectives emerging from this tradition, what is common to all of these views is that they consider knowledge to be extrinsic to the learner. In other words the learner is a blank slate or an empty vessel into which prescribed, externally generated knowledge is inculcated by externally, pre-defined controlled means. Thus, a quality education is determined by the measurement of behaviour/achievement against standardized outcomes complete with a carrot and stick remuneration system.

It is assumed that the large-scale standardized tests, or what are commonly referred to as "high-stake tests," are designed by a-political and neutral experts who make every effort to ensure that their particular biases/values (political, social, gender, sexual, cultural, religious, etc.) do not influence the exams. It is also assumed that all students who study the prescribed materials and who work hard enough will be able to respond to the tests in an identical manner. Furthermore, it is assumed that the tests will be evaluated or assessed by value-neutral machines owned by value-neutral companies (corporations). Thus, every effort is made to ensure that no subjective values or biases creep into and contaminate the assessment process. Finally, it is assumed that those who emerge from this testing process successfully have achieved a standard universal measure of excellence and will be able to perform equally well in their professions and vocations. However, as we pointed out in Chapter 3 during our analysis of Levy-Bruhl, such assumptions ignore the plethora of social and cultural influences affecting students outside white middle-class and upper middle-class norms. There are profound problems with test validity when the cultural specifics of other groups and the subjectivities of individuals are ignored.

Two other problems are immediately apparent in the assumptions behind determining educational excellence. First, both students and their intellectual abilities are treated in much the same manner as objects in natural science research. In other words, students and their intellectual abilities are treated as static educational data that inevitably yields standard results under given circumstances or conditions, and within any given context. Second, it is assumed that internal and external conditions such as psychological, ethnic, sexual, gender, political, and economic contexts do not have any direct bearing on students who are tested for their knowledge through a standardized exam at a particular time and date. Instead, those with a testing fetish view students and teachers as widgets on an educational assembly line who are assessed regularly as part of a quality control protocol.

These assumptions are contestable on a number of grounds. For example, it has been amply illustrated, as we pointed out in our discussion of Levy-Bruhl and that we discuss again later in this chapter, that all standardized testing whether in the form of IQ tests, language tests (e.g. TOEFL) or aptitude tests (GMAT, GRE, LSAT) are inevitably value laden. Such tests are designed with latent cultural, class, and ethnic biases and only those students who have acquired certain assumed cultural capital will consistently perform well on them. Furthermore, the quality of education determined on the basis of these tests is far from a universally agreed-upon model; they do not even meet the criteria of objectivity on which they are supposedly based.

Normative assumptions on worthwhile educational aims and objectives are based on different priorities held by different stakeholders. These stakeholders typically have powerful political or economic reasons for adopting positions on what students ought to learn and how they ought to learn it. Indeed, the normative assumptions left unaddressed by empirical research in education often entail presuppositions that reflect political aims related to the desired structure of the social, economic, and vocational realms within which education occurs. What amounts to a quality education from one perspective – that of the Conference Board of Canada (2001), for example – might simply include the efficacious and instrumental preparation of students for existing labour market conditions. On the other hand, a more critical perspective on education advocated by critical theorists such as Henry Giroux (2004) and Stanley Aronowitz (2001), adopting social equality assumptions, seeks to provide students with the tools to transform society toward some form of democratic socialism. Neither position can be demonstrated as empirically "true," or scientific, but instead requires a different type of argument by advancing moral reasons about what constitutes a quality human experience, an acceptable society, some attending conception of the *good life*, and the model of education required to achieve these objectives.

The resurgence of scientism in the form of standardized testing within educational research is based on a particular version of logical positivism/empiricism that favours randomized experimentalization as the highest standard of research. The discourse on quality education, what Stephan Ball (1997) calls a "quality revolution," includes a fetish for organizational and managerial improvement and effectiveness coupled with a movement for individual accountability. This managerial fetish is reminiscent of a culture of surveillance and mistrust that calls for the auditing of individuals at almost all levels of education: teachers, students, board members, and administrators.

Reminiscent of Herbert Spencer's original motivation, the basic idea behind the current testing drive is that better science will produce better education, that "quality" science will enable us to finally re-engineer education and educational institutions to make them more effective and efficient. However, as Sroufe (1997) argues, "what educational researchers cannot do is compete head to head with the intrinsic glamour of the engineering and biological sciences which seems to be the desire of some 'soft' social scientists trying earnestly to be 'hard' " (p. 26). Schwandt (2005) puts the point this way:

> The American Psychological Association is practically ecstatic at the prospect of an increased role for psychology in establishing the scientific basis for educational interventions in testing, motivation, classroom management, reading instruction, math instruction, preschool curriculum, and character development and socialization of school children. (p.286)

Grover Whitehurst, the director of the Institute of Educational Science of the Department of Education made this point explicitly in one of his recent presentations:

> Psychologists are more likely than any other professional group working in the schools to have scientific training – and respect and understanding of the role of research and evidence in practice – they should be prepared to play an important role in moving the culture of education towards reliance on evidence. (Cited in Schwandt, 2005, p. 286)

Such reification of scientism provides the base on which recent legislation in Great Britain and the USA is enacted. For example, the NCLB document contains as many as 111 references to "scientifically-based research" (St. Pierre, 2006). The NCLB Act borrows its orientation toward scientism from the Reading Excellence Act (REA) of 1999 (this act was repealed with the enactment of NCLB in 2002). The Reading Excellence Act articulates scientific research as follows:

> The term 'scientifically based reading research' (A) means the application of rigorous, systematic, and objective procedures to obtain valid knowledge relevant to reading development, reading instruction, and reading difficulties, and (B) shall include research that – (i) employs systematic, empirical methods that draw on observation or experiment; (ii) involves rigorous data analysis that are adequate to test the stated hypotheses and justify the general conclusions drawn; (iii) relies on measurements or observational methods that provide valid data across evaluators and observers and across multiple measurements and

observations; and (iv) has been accepted by a peer-reviewed journal or approved by a panel of independent experts through a comparably rigorous, objective, and scientific review. (Sweet as cited in St. Pierre, 2006, p. 244)

A later publication by the National Research Council (NRC) reiterated that while it is "possible to describe the physical and social world scientifically so that, for example, multiple observers can agree on what they see," they totally rejected the "postmodern school of thought when it posits that social science researchers can never generate objective or trustworthy knowledge" (NRC, 2002, p. 25). It is interesting to note the narrow way in which the NRC characterizes vehement opposition to scientism as restricted to the postmodernist school of thought. According to the NRC "this description (of the postmodern school of thought) applies to an extreme epistemological perspective that questions the rationality of the scientific enterprise altogether, and instead believes that all knowledge is based on sociological factors like power, influence, and economic factors" (NCR, 2002, p. 25).

One of the centrepieces of the scientifically based research is the verifiability of collected data. For example, an NRC (2005) document titled *Advancing Scientific Research in Education* emphasizes the sharing of data among researchers. The authors of the document, however, seem oblivious to several key points: First, educational researchers, especially those working within postpositivist traditions and with qualitative methodologies, work with various research strategies. Their data collection methods include personal interviews, biography, art work, performance recordings, and a wide range of other approaches. No other researcher can use this data to achieve the same conclusions because they are not empirically verifiable or generalizable in the scientific sense; second, there is a set of research ethics that governs data gathering of human beings and its subsequent usage. Researchers cannot violate the confidence of their research subjects by making available either their narratives or their identities without explicit authorization to those beyond the specific research enterprise; third, narrative data often reflect a subjective discursive context that is potentially meaningless in the intellectual or epistemological context of another researcher, or in a LPE tradition. Finally, generalizability is not the goal of qualitative postpositivist data collection. The validity of collected data is local and even personal, an obviously limiting feature of this research approach when its general contribution to education is assessed.

Of course, the standards-based and scientific research discourse has a definitive preference for anti-qualitative research. Qualitative narratives are opposed because they do not have rival accounts, they are not generalizable, and cannot be replicated or verified. In short, the anti-qualitative/anti-narrative bias of the scientific research discourse can be summed up as follows: (1) narratives do not have rival accounts; (2) they are not generalizable; (3) they cannot be replicated; and (4) they cannot be empirically verified. Faced with this context, Patti Lather (2004) suggests that the US Federal attempt to legislate the scientific method into education should be read as a backlash against the proliferation of research approaches of the last 20 years out of cultural studies, feminist methodologies, radical environmentalists, ethnic studies, and social studies of science – a backlash wherein, under the guise of objectivity and science, colonial, Western, masculine, white, and other biases are adopted. Lather further asserts that the US government, encouraged by its success in controlling reading research, is now targeting fields such as math, science, professional development, and comprehensive school reform as its next objects of high scientific standards with random field trials. As a result, she claims that educational research has become a partisan instrumental tool just as standardized tests became a tool to marginalize certain students in the past.

According to Lather (2004), a net result of such legislative and discursive construction of educational research is that:

> Values and politics, human volition and program variability, cultural diversity, multiple disciplinary perspectives, the import of partnerships with practitioners, even the ethical considerations of random designs: all are swept away in a unified theory of scientific advancement with its mantra of 'science is science is science' across the physical, life, and social sciences. (p.19)

The very complexity of research relationships makes it impossible to replicate, validate, generalize, and objectify any research. In this sense educational research requires much more than just the empirical evidence vehemently advocated by the standards-based research discourse. Empirical evidence in this respect is broadly defined as scientific research in fields such as psychology, sociology, neuroscience, and economics. Scientific research in education is defined as replication of such research in educational contexts "wherein objective measures of performance are used to compare, evaluate, and monitor progress" (Schwandt, 2005, p. 292).

Although we greatly sympathize with many of the legitimate concerns raised by Lather and other postmodernists, their defence of qualitative research does not address the fact that such practices have contributed virtually nothing to the improvement of teaching and learning. If education research is simply a forum for alternative voices, it hardly warrants the millions of research dollars annually invested in the field. Such a worthwhile but separate mission requires developing better forums for social activism rather than using education "research" as a vehicle for airing marginalized voices.

4.3   The Problem of Researcher Bias

We pointed out in Chapter 2 that the attempt to improve education through organized science has persisted since the mid nineteenth century so that the problem of scientism, although intensified by recent initiatives, is not an especially new development. And yet, in spite of the long-standing faith in science, there is precious little to show for more than 150 years of scientific inquiry into the field of education. Driven by his commitment to the ill-fated recapitulation theory and his distorted understanding of evolutionary biology, even in the case of Herbert Spencer it is obvious that the primary factor influencing research findings was the underlying assumptions of the researcher.

The normative biases of researchers and scholars within education are apparent in a range of areas. For example, the dominance of learner-centred pedagogy, emerging from the progressive education movement of the early twentieth century, inevitably shapes education and classroom instruction in particular sorts of ways. Correspondingly, researchers approaching classroom observation and analysis from a student-centred perspective, or what in contemporary educational jargon is referred to as constructivism, will evaluate their observations through a preconceived framework privileging this type of pedagogical interaction. A researcher accepting the assumptions related to subject-centred learning, on the other hand, will adopt a different set of presuppositions to impose on the observed phenomena. As a result, the subsequent conclusions drawn will feature contrary observations and research findings regarding the effectiveness of classroom design. One researcher may use student/teacher interaction as the appropriate measure of classroom success while another researcher measures propositional knowledge to assess education quality. Our point here is simply that different types of presuppositions regarding learning practices and educational outcomes are apt to result in radically different analyses of the same collected data. In education, the means and ends are intrinsically connected.

Often these underlying philosophies shape the very nature and focus of the conducted research. For example, although progressive education has been accused of being pedagogically ineffective (see, e.g. Hirsch, 2001; Ravitch, 2000), effectiveness in this sense is largely measured by student acquisition of propositional knowledge measured quantitatively through various testing protocols. If the question of pedagogical effectiveness is expanded or transformed to include dispositional outcomes as they relate to democratic citizenship, an entirely different evaluation of progressive practices is forthcoming (Hyslop-Margison & Richardson, 2005; Hyslop-Margison & Sears, 2006). From a democratic perspective, the focus is shifted from the mere acquisition of propositional knowledge to one that enhances the political voice of students.

To carry this point further, in the evaluation and measurement of effectiveness as it relates to democratic citizenship, the units (central concepts) of analysis are not necessarily observable or objectively measurable in the sense that the standards-based research discourse proposes. A democratic classroom, among other things, will largely depend on the creation of a learning space that is open, hospitable, and has expanded boundaries for discourse (Palmer, 1993). It will also depend on how the personal truths of the teacher interact with those of the learners regarding factors such as the ability of teachers to authentically engage with and share their inner landscape, or what Maykut and Moorehouse (1994) call emotional and intellectual baggage.

The effectiveness of educational research that seeks to gauge the democratic effectiveness of a classroom in creating democratic subjects will depend largely on the epistemological position from which the researcher proceeds and on attending normative assumptions. The methods used to "measure" the effectiveness will largely emanate from these two factors. Let us employ an example of two researchers both aiming to "measure" the effectiveness of the classroom with respect to democratic citizenship. Let us suppose one of them adheres to the standards-based research model while the second researcher is oriented toward postpositivistic perspectives (we are using postpositivist in a broad and general sense). The standards-based researcher will focus on enumerating indicators such as how many times students are permitted to question information or provide input on the subject matter. If all or even a majority of students get equal time and if the numbers suggest that students do get the opportunity to question the material, the probable conclusion is that the classroom is democratic.

On the other hand, the researcher operating from a non-positivist perspective will be more interested in examining what kind of a physical and emotional space is being created in the classroom; what kind of topics are discussed and what type of contestations take place? How do the teacher and the students enact social and intellectual boundaries within which their respective views engage each other? These methods, and the alternative assumptions they entail, may lead to a different conclusion on the democratic nature of the same classroom.

As educators and researchers, humans are not valueless beings who view the world in a phenomenological fashion devoid of conceptual and normative presuppositions. Rather, our previous life experiences, the class, ethnicity, sexual and gendered context from which we emerge, and the environment we presently inhabit all operate to shape our worldview in very particular sorts of ways. From the selection of a research topic to the interpretation of research findings, a researcher's context and biases inevitably influence his or her findings and related claims about preferred classroom practice.

The author's personal experiences and situation frequently influence the research findings in education. In a manual on research design, for example, Denzin and Lincoln (1998) observe that, "Interpretive research begins and ends with the biography and self of the researcher" (p. 12). This observation reflects the recognition that an individual's research interests are driven by a particular normative or ideological bias that is embodied both within the chosen area of research and in the interpretation of the collected data. It seems rather obvious that neither students nor academic researchers normally pursue a topic unless it resonates with their own political agenda or has some relevance to their personal experience. A researcher's personal beliefs and values are reflected in method selection, the interpretation of findings and in the choice of a research topic.

What a researcher believes in a normative, philosophical, or even metaphysical sense (in the case of religious presuppositions) more or less determines what subject, issue, or problem is selected for study and may accordingly influence the interpretation of the collected data. The traditional positivist research paradigm widely applied in the study of education has misguidedly led researchers to assume tacitly that what they are studying often has no personal significance or is disconnected from their personal feelings and inclinations. From a scientific perspective, of course, the only acceptable reason directing a particular research project in education is intellectual curiosity and the "improvement" of classroom practice. But more often than not, personal beliefs and views about a topic – either in support of one side of the argument or on the social, cultural, political subtexts – guide the development and direction of the attending inferences and argument.

In support of these various observations, Scheurich (1997) argues that one's historical position, one's class (which may or may not include changes over the course of a lifetime), race, gender, religion, and so on – all of these interact and influence, limit and constrain the production of "knowledge." In addition to one's social and historical positioning, a researcher's evolving self in terms of the deliberate educational and professional choices made throughout an academic career also influence the selection of a research topic. For example, an academic who has chosen educational psychology as a career will pursue knowledge through the accepted methods and practices of that particular field. A proponent of Piaget's theory will interpret observations through a conceptual lens that supports developmental learning while a Marxist might see all observed data as a manifestation of class struggle and economic inequality. In light of these academic commitments, then, researchers choose to study a particular topic in education because they see some personal relevance to it either as a practitioner or situated individual carrying particular types of experiential and academic baggage. Given the range of various human predispositions, the potential for eliminating bias as required by purely scientific investigation appears exceptionally limited.

From the choice of the research project to the choice of methodological strategies, the researcher is guided by beliefs that in turn depend upon his or her positioning in an interlocking web of experiences including history, gender, sexual orientation, ethnicity, religion etc. The process through which the research progresses is dependent on the beliefs and positionality of the research subjects. For example, Nias (1993) researched teachers' lives, life histories, and careers with a set of assumptions and methods based on these assumptions only to discover that her assumptions about primary teachers needed to be altered.

Nias' research project grew out of her experience at the school of education at Liverpool University where she was responsible for designing and running a 1-year postgraduate certificate in education. To situate herself and her research Nias writes:

> Each year there was a substantial cohort of secondary students: the primary group numbered between 12 and 20 and worked in an isolated basement in a large old building whose upper floors were inhabited by more prestigious courses. As a result, we spent many hours in each other's company and got to know each other well. Once individuals had begun teaching, they would often telephone, call or write. When, one day, someone who had been teaching for three years returned from many miles away to talk about her experiences in school I decided to spend a forthcoming sabbatical term visiting past graduates from this course. (1993, p.133)

As mentioned earlier, Nias went to the field with a predetermined research schema in mind. However, as she puts it, "almost as soon as I began to talk to them I realized that many of my concerns were of little relevance or importance to them. Instead they wanted to talk to me about what they were doing now and about their pressing memories of earlier encounters with adults in school, not just their pupils" (p. 133). Taking into account the narratives of her research subjects led Nias to alter the orientation of her research project. In other words the interests and values of the subjects of research engaged with that of the researcher to alter the research topic as well as the process and eventual outcomes of the research.

Now consider what would happen if the same research project was undertaken from a standards-based or scientific research perspective. The researcher would have gone to the field with a predetermined hypothesis (based on previous research by others in the field) a prepared instrument, for example, a survey, questionnaire, etc. or observed teachers in a controlled environment, and on the basis of gathered data would have concluded if the hypothesis was proved or disproved. In either case the voices of the research subjects, the people who actually work in and with the system would have no bearing on the educational research conducted.

The evidence that researcher bias creeps into supposedly empirical and objective claims is ubiquitous throughout education research. The NCLB conviction, unfortunately one increasingly adopted by the Canadian public education system as evidenced by recent policies implemented in New Brunswick, Alberta, and Ontario, that standardized testing offers an empirical method to measure the quality of public schools and teacher competence represents one troubling example of this problem. The advocates of standardized testing, and the scientism it entails, assume that high scores on standardized tests equate to successful academic and learning experiences, including quality instruction, while low scores are supposedly indicative of school failure, teacher incompetence, and administrative misdirection. NCLB, a classic example of what is wrong with thinking about education rather than a reasoned remedy to improve its quality, boldly proclaims, for example, that:

> The data will be available in annual report cards on school performance and on state wide progress. They will give parents information about the quality of their children's schools, the qualifications of their teachers, and their children's progress in key subjects. (NCLB, 2000)

Millions of federal dollars are invested annually in the USA at the state and federal levels based entirely on assumptions that are driven by extremely narrow conceptions of what constitutes educational and teacher quality.

The form of standardized testing reflected in NCLB, however well intentioned (although we suspect its motivation to be somewhat less than noble as we point out later in the text), operationally defines quality learning by testing student recall of a relatively narrow band of provided information. The higher cognitive capacities of imagination, creativity, and critically thinking, or the participatory dispositions required for democratic citizenship, are ignored by the assessment approach. The assumption that high-test scores on narrow standardized tests that measure propositional knowledge equate to a quality education is, quite clearly, a problematic one. As we pointed out in Chapter 2, many of the so-called empirical practices within education attempt to answer philosophical questions rather than empirical ones. The matter of measuring what constitutes a quality education through standardized testing procedures affords yet another example of this prevalent error in current research and assessment practices.

In fairness to current standardized testing proponents, this same problem is present regardless of the conception of education and whatever corresponding testing methods are employed. Suppose, for example, we wanted to measure citizenship education based on the view that a good citizen is a compliant, passive individual who obeys all laws and votes without exception at all formal electoral events for which he or she is eligible. The testing might be based on self-reporting of learned dispositions or some other more complicated testing procedure with accompanying statistical methods – for example, regression analysis or sampling theory – that supposedly account for a range of individual variables.

Those completing such a study would ultimately draw inferences based on the provided responses and their subsequent data analysis. Regardless of the testing outcomes, an appropriate concept of citizenship is one that must be identified through philosophical discussion. It cannot be determined by empirical testing. Citizenship, similar to what constitutes a quality education, is inevitably a contested concept open to a range of assumptions and perspectives. For example, rather than a law abiding, socially compliant individual who votes every 4 years, a good citizen might be alternatively defined as someone involved in social change, resists dominant and oppressive social trends, and exercises his or her political voice through popular activism instead of simply at the ballot box. Rather than routinely obeying all laws regardless of their implications, a good citizen might be defined as someone who breaks laws that are deemed patently unfair or unjust.

It is precisely such debate and contestation over meaning making in educational research that the standards-based research movement seeks to undermine by emphasizing value-neutral "scientific" educational research. The scientism inherent in current policy initiatives across the Western world minimize the role of researchers' values in educational research and, therefore, stifle debate on conceptual matters. As a result, current and dominant values – primarily neo-liberal ones – remain largely unchallenged.

The widespread advocacy of instrumentalism is visible at two different levels: (1) as Fredrick Erickson (2005) points out, instrumental objectives are achieved through an illustrative list of potential research topics for educational research that aims to exclude descriptive and normative research and thus also the chances of researchers' normative perspectives creeping into the research process. The emphasis is placed on research topics (or fields) that call for some sort of causal analysis with the ends simply assumed; (2) in terms of the questions that the current standards-based research promotes, descriptive and normative questions are severely limited. For example, as Erikson argues, three types of questions at the heart of standards based research: "what is happening (concerning description), "does x cause y?" (identification of cause), and "why does x cause y?" (concerning explanation of causal relations) (2005, p. 7). He argues that by focusing on (and prescribing by means of grants, patronage, etc.) causal questions, standards-based research aims to exclude research approaches that challenge prevailing norms and values. In other words, standards-based research strips social science research of its qualitative and normative analytic agenda.

Erikson (2005) suggests the tendency in current educational research is one that "privileges questions of efficiency and effectiveness over questions of hermeneutical or critical description and analysis by what it silences implicitly through omission as well as by what it says explicitly – completes the disadvantaging of interpretive and critical studies in education, marginalizing as well those of feminist research, history, and philosophy" (p. 8). Scientific research in education, especially in the area of academic achievement, then, inevitably begins with tacit value judgements concerning curriculum aims, contestable concepts and educational quality, and then interprets collected data based on those assumptions. As we pointed out earlier, the NCLB conviction that standardized testing offers an empirical, scientific method to measure the quality of public schools and teacher competence simply represents one case in point.

In addition to the narrow construal of quality education, there is no attention paid to the other variables that impact on student academic achievement and attainment, most notably of course social and economic status. Indeed, a student's social and economic status far outreaches any other variable besides perhaps direct and positive parental involvement as the principle force correlating with academic achievement and attainment (Pratt, 1994). Somehow, this important bit of empirical evidence conveniently gets lost in the various initiatives launched by the NRC and NCLB.

To reiterate our critical point, educational researchers are not, and probably can never be, objectively detached from their subject of study because their normative perspectives, career orientation, and preconceptions bear directly on their selection and evaluation of the studied phenomena. For example, how many educational researchers simply report quantitative or even qualitative data without making normative inferences about their findings? How many of the conclusions drawn are clearly reflected in the collected data? These questions are difficult ones to answer and, without detached third party intervention in education research, definitive answers are nearly impossible to provide.

In those rare cases where normative inferences are not made, the assumptions are often embedded in the observed educational circumstances. If researchers explore whether community involvement by students promotes student participation at the ballot box, for example, they have already assumed that formal political participation in voting exercises is equivalent to a successful model of citizenship. Why else, of course, would they conduct such research? Hence, the assumptions may be explicit or tacit but they inevitably influence empirical research in education in a variety of important ways. In the final analysis, one cannot perform empirical research in education without such assumptions and these assumptions require a sophisticated supporting argument that is too often lacking or entirely absent.

The stakes for teachers, administrators, students, and schools subjected to the type of evaluations that adopt such normative assumptions related to quality educational experiences are extremely high with dismissals and resource reductions the potential consequences of legislation such as NCLB. In addition to NCLB's absolute lack of appreciation for contextual variability in causal relationships between teaching and learning, the presumption that standardized tests effectively measure quality learning presupposes without warrant or argument (a move typical in scientism) that high empirically measured testing outcomes equate to educational excellence and, even more important for teachers, quality instruction. The absence of philosophical argument to support underlying normative assumptions also promotes instrumental reasoning that insulates existing social, economic, and educational practices from meaningful critique. Contrary to the assumptions adopted by NCLB advocates, Noddings (2004) contends that standardized tests "are loaded with trivia" and students are "being fed intellectual junk food" (p. 494) to succeed on these tests. As Lather notes, "formulas for transparent accountability are more about politics than about quality of service" (2004, p. 20).

As we have already pointed out, the variable of social–economic status correlates (SES) most highly with student academic achievement (Sadovnik et al., 2001), an empirical finding that seriously undermines the assumptions of NCLB that blame administrators, teachers, and schools for low academic achievement. The inference that standardized tests measure the quality of education obviously involves a non-empirical, value saturated, and non-argued assumption, but it provides the political architects of NCLB and other similar policies with an effective ideological mechanism to castigate schools, teachers, and administrators for outcomes that are frequently beyond their personal or collective control. The micro-level accountability measures advanced by NCLB effectively deflect public and political attention away from the profound structural injustices within American society that actually precipitate low levels of academic achievement and attainment among many economically disadvantaged students. The ideological advantages of scientism to the prevailing hegemony will be fully discussed in Chapter 6, but our critically important present point is that the "problems" of education are, more often than not, simply manifestations of structural issues.

The equating of high-test scores with some peculiar kind of educational nirvana and teacher mastery is not only a normative judgement, as Noddings' and Lather's comments suggest, it is a judgement based on an extraordinarily narrow view of what constitutes a quality learning experience and what factors influence student learning. This assessment approach pleads blind and rather unforgivable ignorance to the social and cultural factors that confront many highly committed teaching professionals on a daily basis. All of these factors shape the context of classroom instruction and inevitably influence academic outcomes. Standardized tests provide an operational definition of quality schooling, then, while simultaneously distracting researchers, parents, the public, and politicians from the structural injustices that impact deleteriously and broadly on student academic success. Meanwhile, there is very little, if any, attending discourse by government officials on how to correct the economic injustices correlated to academic achievement and attainment.

A purely empirical assessment, devoid of normative assumptions, of student learning would provide rather unspectacular results. For example, standardized tests that respect Weber's value-neutral social scientific principles would simply report rather mundane and trivial propositional claims such as x scored 75% and y scored 35% on a particular testing procedure. Instead, the inferences emerging from this type of assessment data – that x is enjoying a quality educational experience while y is suffering the effects of teacher incompetence and school inadequacy – are not scientific, empirical, intersubjective, or educationally productive. As we have demonstrated in Chapter 3, the cultural biases embedded in such tests are also cause for genuine concern in terms of their overall validity. These tests are based instead on an aberrant mix of empirical observations, normative assumptions, and cultural bias, and from our perspective rather conspicuous ideological agendas.

The empirical research approaches employed to measure student achievement, then, begin with narrow normative assumptions about what constitutes quality learning experiences and extend these assumptions into subsequent non-empirical inferences. These problematic assumptions, which similarly support practices of intelligence and SAT testing in academics, are never scientifically instantiated but always normative and most frequently tacit in nature. However, the veneer of science cast over this type of research lends these practices an undeserved air of objectivity and, within a milieu marked by unquestioned faith in the merits of scientific rationality, convinces the general public of the ability of science to measure and improve teaching and learning.

While there are numerous advantages for the corporate world, especially the publishing and the testing industry in the legislation and implementation of science-based research, the negative consequences of such research for the field of education merit serious consideration. The ideological and ethical dimensions of mass testing, or what Peter McLaren (2003) terms "high-stakes testing," cannot be morally ignored. In educational systems where high-stakes testing has been implemented the entire preoccupation of the teachers is preparing students for such tests. The future of both the students and the teachers is often dependent upon the scores achieved on these tests. This fetish for testing corresponds with the shrinking of time and space available for engaging with issues related to the interlocking structural questions related to ethnicity, class, gender, sexual orientation, and democratic citizenship. In other words less and less time and learning are earmarked for discussion of these and other critical or democratic issues. As Amy Gluckman (cited by McLaren, 2003, p. 45) argues:

> Drop out rates among African-American and Latino students have risen since high-stakes testing began. There is even some evidence that students who pass the TAAS (Texas Assessment of Academic Skills) test and graduate actually demonstrate poorer writing skills when they arrive at college than did their peers a few years earlier, before high stakes testing.

To summarize our major points in this section; since teachers inevitably teach to the test, especially so when the stakes for their professional careers are so enormously high, students end up receiving a narrow band of information and restricted learning that may very well retard their overall academic growth and intellectual development. It almost certainly limits the amount of time spent on discussion of critical and/or democratic issues in the classroom. Indeed, the stakes for students, teachers, and schools in standards-based assessment within the USA and elsewhere are enormously high with retention, dismissals, and resource reductions the potential consequence for everyone involved. As Amy Gluckman points out, the evidence suggesting high stakes testing is improving academic performance is questionable at best.

In addition to the total disregard for contextual variability in causal relationships between teaching, learning, and academic outcomes embedded within such testing practices, the assumption that standardized testing measures quality learning presupposes without warrant or argument that testing outcomes equate to educational excellence and quality instruction. This is yet another negative and distorting outcome of scientism in education that simply perpetuates a form of instrumental learning that neglects the important foundational questions essential to more democratic forms of teaching and learning.

4.4   Conceptual Confusion and Construct Validity

The terms employed throughout education and within educational research often tend to be poorly defined and reflect unstated assumptions and objectives regarding educational experiences. School psychologists, for example, spend a significant amount of time identifying students as "gifted" or in less-flattering cases as "slow learners." But what do these terms actually mean in relation to human experience? The measures for giftedness include a range of tests that largely mimic the academic expectations of contemporary schooling, a feature that affords them status as good "predictors" of academic success. In some cases, students are asked questions in a manner similar to equally problematic IQ tests that require exposure to certain cultural experiences that many students simply may not access. Consequently, student inability to answer such questions successfully is not necessarily a function of some internal intellectual deficit, but rather the outcome of particular cultural contexts where exposure to the tested concepts is denied. The problem of conceptual ambiguity and questions of construct validity undermine other concepts in education, including critical thinking and creativity that are largely reduced to the realm of educational slogans. A slogan is simply a term that has widespread popular appeal, but offers little or nothing in terms of actual pedagogical substance.

Intelligence aside, a child growing up in a wealthy upper middle-class environment with access to books, concepts, and discussions related to questions that require the kind of cultural knowledge frequently denied poor children will inevitably achieve higher scores on most academic tests. But is this a function of some innate ability as the concepts of "giftedness" and "slow learner" imply? Some students may be far enough removed from academic culture outside the school that they will be labeled as learning disabled. Such labels, of course, adhere to students throughout their schooling experience, influencing expectations and opportunities, and set off a range of subsequent events in education that may profoundly limit future academic achievement (Sadovnik et al.). One troubling example of this problem provided by Barrow (1995) in his trenchant critique of the process of intelligence testing, and related types of testing such as SATs and their potentially biased implications, elucidates this point nicely:

> One SAT item requires individuals to choose between four alternatives the pattern that is analogous to the pattern of runner/marathon. The choice lies between (a) Envoy/embassy; (b) martyr/massacre; (c) oarsman/regatta; and (d) referee/tournament. The testers proclaim the correct answer to be (c) oarsmen/regatta. It will be argued by many that this is a highly debatable contention. More to the immediate point, can one seriously maintain there is no

cultural bias here? Is everybody as familiar with the idea of regattas and oarsmen as everyone
else? Was there never a person whose upbringing and background left him or her unfamiliar
with words like envoy and embassy? (p. 292)

The answers to the questions Barrow rightfully raises are as obvious as the serious
validity problems present within these tests. Clearly, such tests measure a combination of cultural exposure to certain concepts and the predisposition of students to
apply those concepts in a manner consistent with those deemed appropriate by the
test designers. We may surmise with some measure of confidence that children
from New York's Harlem district and or the Watts district of Los Angeles will
generally have had little exposure to terms such as regatta and oarsmen while those
living in Florida's West Palm Beach or Massachusetts' Martha's Vineyard may be
very familiar with these terms.

If the test involved concepts and experiences limited to African-American inner
city children, as we argued through the work of Levy-Bruhl in Chapter 3, the results
would clearly indicate very different outcomes. Here again, however, the principles
of scientific investigation as a set of empirically testable questions are forced on a
context where they are fundamentally inapplicable, or at least applicable in a very
narrow sense. Indeed, they obviously measure something, but why should we
believe or agree that what they measure is innate intelligence? And yet, the labels,
some of them quite damaging to a learner's self-image and how he or she is per-
ceived by others, that emerge from these tests are applied to students and influence
the remainder of their academic and schooling trajectory.

The type of "intelligence" required to excel in academics is fundamentally
different from that required to survive as a single parent African-American living
in the Los Angeles Watts district or as a Canadian aboriginal person living on a
federal reserve. We ought to understand that within education our applied mechanisms are imbued with normative presuppositions about the qualities valued by our
cultural context and our testing simply measures how close students come to meeting that particular set of assumptions. At the core of this problem is a point we have
repeated throughout the previous narrative – that many of the questions researchers
in education seek to answer through empirical or "scientific" inquiry are not really,
at their root, empirical questions at all.

The entire field of giftedness in education is perhaps even more wrought with
conceptual confusions and cultural bias than intelligence testing. Even in advance
of such conceptual ambiguity, there is, as we know, a powerful correlation
between social economic class and those students who are identified as gifted.
Although we do not claim this injustice as the sole determinant of academic
achievement, this correlation should raise immediate concerns that a child's
enhanced ability to read, apply concepts, and perform other academic skills is often
the result of a privileged social and economic background, a range of learning
advantages related to economic privilege, and the exposure to cultural capital that
such privilege typically provides.

We are not denying here the possibility of some biological component determining
disparate levels of academic skills and abilities between individuals, but it is easy
to overrate this component while simultaneously disregarding the cultural and

personal barriers to intellectual culture and academic achievement. Even if the biological argument is accepted, it does not resolve the important normative question of whether particular qualities are reflective of "intelligence," an issue that involves an entirely different set of philosophical questions and arguments.

There is, then, a fundamental problem in determining what qualities ought to designate a person as being properly identified as "gifted." For example, there is no accounting in present tests for groups of children who may possess exceptional abilities outside the basic range of academic and culturally specific skills assessed by current testing procedures. Neither is there an effective mechanism in such testing to distinguish between giftedness and simple cultural advantage where some children have far greater access to the intellectual capital consistent with that required for academic success.

The concept of giftedness earmarks some students for aggressive academic challenges through various enrichment programmes, namely those with distinct socio-economic advantages, while simultaneously ignoring other abilities that make students uniquely talented in some unmeasured capacity. One empirical claim related to pedagogy clearly indicates that high expectations impact directly on student achievement (Pratt, 1994). Once again, educational psychology provides us with an operational definition of giftedness that defines the concept as someone who does well on the corresponding tests. However, the notion that such empirical tests identify some pre-existing naturally occurring category of so-called giftedness is wrought with profound conceptual, epistemological, and philosophical error. Giftedness is a social construct and derivative of subjectively determined qualities and not an assessment of some ontological quality identified through empirical testing.

Obviously, a reasonable and objective scientific language must be clear and unambiguous, and represent as accurately as possible naturally occurring states of affairs in the world. Even operational definitions must be clearly defined and justified as appropriate. The language or discourse in education, however, is dominated by sloppy sloganizing and conceptual ambiguities. Put another way, the statements of a truly scientific language must qualify as propositions in that their truth or falsity is determined by strict observational rather than entirely normative means, or by judgements that precede the application of operational definitions.

Even within behaviourism, thought by many to be the hardest of the soft psychological sciences, the language and concepts remain dangerously ambiguous and prone to normative judgement. For example, Thornkdike's (1898) *Law of Effect* states that positively reinforced behaviour will be repeated with greater frequency, or if the behaviour is negatively reinforced it will be eventually extinguished. In a clearly scientific language there ought to be clarification of what specific behaviour is being referred to, what specific forces constitute reinforcement (both positive or negative), and what the environmental constants are, for example, the appearance and structure of the maze through which the rats must travel to trigger the reinforcement. When behaviourism is applied to classroom situations, the identification of these constants becomes virtually impossible given the range of potential variables involved.

Even at the seemingly unsophisticated level of laboratory rats, the terms "positive" and "negative" tend to promote a certain measure of subjectivity in interpretation. Positive and negative reinforcements are far less empirical descriptors than they are potential normative judgements evaluating the effects of external stimuli. The subjective nature of such terms means that universal predictions of behaviour are impossible based on the *Law of Effect* since the key terms on which the theory is based are always open to subjective interpretation. Will all rats inevitably act the same under identical circumstances or might their responses be different from the general conclusions drawn by a limited range of experiments? In humans, of course, with our inherent degree of subjective complexity, the concepts of positive and negative reinforcement become even more problematic and are apt to reflect potentially contradictory sets of behaviour describing exactly the same stimulus.

A sadomasochist or someone of similar inclination, for example, would not interpret negative reinforcement in the form of inflicted pain in a manner similar to a physically sensitive person who abhors any and all levels of personal discomfort. To employ an example directly from education: Is ejecting a troublesome student from the classroom a negative or positive reinforcer? Some students inevitably view such dismissal as a reward for inappropriate classroom behaviour. There is another serious problem with Thorndike's *Law of Effect* in that its implications or findings are logically analytic, a problem we will expand upon considerably during our discussion in Chapter 5.

The conceptual ambiguity in social science can be illustrated with another example, albeit from a different social science discipline and in a different context than education. When Robert McNamara, a cabinet member of both the Kennedy and Johnson administrations tried to apply economic "laws" to human beings, the results were disastrous. During the Vietnam War Robert McNamara, a leading economist and then Secretary of State applied the economics "law of firms" which holds that if costs are raised too high for firms they behave in one of the two ways: either they fold up and go out of business or they merge with the larger firm. However, when McNamara and his economic whiz-kids applied this law to break the will of the Vietcong they failed to factor-in the human will. The Vietcong did not behave as a firm because the high human cost was still not high enough when compared to retaining their freedom, sovereignty, and dignity. Extending this example to the field of education, our point is simply that not all "scientific" theorizing in other disciplines including other "scientific" social science disciplines such as psychology, sociology, and economics is helpful in conducting meaningful educational research.

4.5   The Problem of Generalizability

The debate over generalizability in education research is derivative of the basic understanding that a distinctive feature of humankind is the fact that one person differs in fundamental ways from every other person. If this seemingly unproblematic observation is, in fact, the case, then how can a statement about one group of people or a particular individual correctly apply to an entirely different group of persons or another individual?

The solution to this daunting problem advanced by human scientists, including those in educational psychology, involves the introduction of sampling theory and inductive statistics. According to sampling theory, the subjects in any study can be appropriately selected to represent the wider general population: "The process of selecting members of a research sample from a defined population, usually with the intent that the sample accurately represents that population" (Gall et al., 1996, p. 769).

Inductive statistics purportedly calculates the extent to which the relationships within the sample represent the relationships in the general or background population. If we accept the logic and statistical validity of these approaches, of course, a study of 100 different people could be legitimately extended to infer the same relationship within a population of one million. Much of the polling results conducted in advance of electoral processes pursue precisely this type of statistical inference. On the other hand, if we are suspicious about the logic and validity of these statistical practices, then there remains cause for concern over such generalization inferences. The issue of generalizability remains at least an open question within social science research.

The question of generalizability is one that has dogged empirical research in the human sciences for quite some time. In his defense of empirical research, D. C. Phillips (2005) responds to Barrow's (1984) claim that empirical research in education is ungeneralizable because of the infinite range of contextual variables by advancing a rather uncharacteristically weak retort. Phillips defends empirical research against this charge by simply pointing out that there is considerable disagreement among experts in the field on the nature and seriousness of this particular problem:

> There are many anthropologists (including ethnographers) who study humans acting in specific sociological settings, and who claim do to be doing rigorous science – although, crucially, they recognize that this is not science in the positivistic sense of the term. While some social scientists agree that generalization from specific contextualized cases is not possible, there are others who disagree.

Obviously, disagreement between experts in a field of study on such an important issue hardly instils confidence in the particular theory or practice in question. The issue of contextual variables and their impact on empirical findings, then, is worth exploring beyond the cursory defence Phillips provides in his recent apology for empirical research. Also, although we are of course reluctant to engage in *poisoning the well* practices, it is worth noting that Phillips was employed by the National Research Council as part of a committee struck to defend empirical research in education when he wrote the article in question.

We may be able to elucidate our concerns in this area by relating the issue directly to the research within education. In the course of predicting and explaining student behaviour – the inevitable objective of empirical research in education – inferences are invariably made regarding the causal beliefs and desires of students.

To make a certain theory generalizable, these mental states if you will, in terms of both their antecedent causes and pedagogical implications, must be extended beyond individual cases and applied to specific groups with some confidence in their corresponding accuracy.

If a researcher in education claims that collaborative learning enhances student knowledge of algebra, for example, an inference is correspondingly made that collaborative learning experiences generate mental states and character dispositions among students conducive to learning algebra. For empirical research to enjoy this measure of generalizability, then, education must be reducible to explanations about students' beliefs and dispositions, and their universal relationship to particular pedagogical situations. Put even more simply, rather rigid behaviourist presuppositions, those we have addressed and challenged previously in this chapter, must be tacitly advanced by the researchers to make their findings tenable.

There are a number of serious philosophical problems associated with these generalization requirements. Quite clearly, empirical researchers in education may observe specific phenomena but, since they do not have access to other minds, they cannot observe mental states and, hence, non-empirical assumptions about causes, beliefs, and dispositions, and their implications, remain a necessary condition of research that advances pedagogical recommendations on any subject. Obviously, identical observable learning outcomes may result from entirely different non-empirical antecedent causes in the form of specific beliefs or dispositions, and assumptions about uniform antecedent causes, the holy grail of empirical research within education, are therefore fundamentally problematic.

However, it is precisely these elusive generalizations and antecedent causes that empirical research in education must identify to provide educators with the etiological principles that they (and the National Research Council in the USA) seek in order to warrant the resource commitment to pursue the silver bullet notion of "best practice." It is one thing to provide an empirical account of some human phenomenon and quite another to cite the cause of the phenomenon in the subsequent analysis of the observation. It is also one thing to report on the empirical observation of a group of students within a particular context, and quite another thing to extend those observations to a general population of students.

The lack of attention to context, or environmental constants, as we have described them in our analysis of Thorndike's *law of effect*, is a grave problem in empirical research within education. Indeed, no two students or classrooms are identical and what occurs in one context, even as a result of strictly controlled classroom variables might (and often does) lead to an entirely different outcome in another. This makes the possibility of predicting outcomes based on a single or limited series of observations extremely problematic, resulting in the often contradictory claims emerging from educational research. Those of us with considerable teaching experience understand the need to be flexible and reflective even within the same classroom context in our pedagogical approaches precisely for this reason. The positivist assumption that natural constants can be identified may apply very well in analysing organic compounds or geological rock formations, but its ability to capture the complex dynamics of human behaviour remains very much in question.

In the same previously mentioned article in which he defends empirical research in education, D. C. Phillips (2005) singles out a text by Biesta and Burbules (2003) entitled *Pragmatism and Educational Research* for criticism by suggesting that the book offers only a brief and contrived example to support its case against empirical research in education. Phillips neglects to mention, however, that the authors' primary intention in the book is not to launch an attack on empirical research per se, but rather to investigate the possible contributions of pragmatism to the understanding, study, and enhancement of education.

Pragmatism and Educational Research provides readers with a philosophical analysis of pragmatism that includes its implications for educational research based on epistemic limitations. For pragmatists, knowledge is a function of "what works" rather than a scientifically instantiated Archimedean or immutable truth. Specific examples of empirical research would therefore contribute little to the arguments advanced in the text since they are based on the authors' analysis of a specific school of philosophy with its attending epistemological implications. Of course, one obvious implication of pragmatist epistemology identified by the authors and consistent with our analysis in Chapter 2, and also one that apparently troubles Phillips the most, is that a science of education founded on abstract and immutable pedagogical principles is simply impossible because pragmatists understand that, "every situation we encounter [in education] is in some sense unique" (Biesta & Burbules, 2003, p. 110).

The empirical study of education is not entirely meaningless to pragmatists or to us, but given the impact of context on the claims of empirical research any discovered pedagogical implications are inevitably mediated by an almost infinite range of contextual factors. Truth is therefore also contextual. The claim that water boils at 100°C, for example, is only true at sea level and for fresh water, and all truths, according to pragmatists, are subject to similar contextual caveats. The results of empirical research to the pragmatist, then, are not immutable recipes to follow on the path to culinary perfection but very general recipe guides about possible ingredients to include in certain dishes. Hence, empirical research must be interpreted and applied by professional educators as active agents working within a recognized context instead of simply consumed and applied as abstracted pedagogical knowledge.

Of course, we do not wish to dismiss entirely the possibility of making limited claims, rather than sweeping generalizations, on the basis of empirical study. Some limited empirical generalizations, such as conclusions about the effectiveness of whole language versus phoneme instruction for reading, may actually provide limited criteria for causal likelihood, or identify something that operates as a potential causal factor in a significant number of cases. For example, an empirical researcher may legitimately claim that phoneme instruction offers a more effective approach to reading instruction in the hands of a certain type of teacher while instructing a certain type of student with a certain type of reading material and so on. However, we will leave it to the reader to determine the ultimate value of such claims when applied to practical cases of general classroom instruction that are subject to a virtually indeterminate range of classroom variables.

4.6   Same Evidence Leads to Different Conclusions

Another fundamental test of a truly scientific theory requires that different researchers following similar investigative procedures end up with the same conclusion regarding observed phenomena. If there are a multitude of potential or possible explanations for a given phenomenon, for example, how can we conclude that one is scientifically superior, or more truthful, than any other one? However, there is very little reason to believe that the methods of inquiry employed by empirical research in education can be formalized to preclude differing subjective judgements based on pre-existing theoretical or normative commitments. Two researchers adopting dissimilar normative assumptions and opposing theoretical frameworks, while nevertheless employing rigorous empirical methods of inquiry and data collection, may reach radically different conclusions – recall the Gestalt switch referred to by Kuhn where one's perspective changes between identifying a duck and a rabbit as an analogy for the type of problem at hand – when investigating exactly the same phenomenon. In other words, two researchers may agree on all of the observable facts (in the case of the rabbit/duck profile this might include the curvature of the lines, their length etc.), but interpret those facts on the basis of distinct fundamental presuppositions that lead them to disparate inferences and conclusions.

Let us suppose, for example, that instead of observing children's learning through a stage development model such as that proposed by Piaget, researchers adopt epistemological presuppositions derived from Vygotsky for understanding the basis of learner development. Vygotsky suggests that learning drives development rather than the other way around (Maxwell, 2004), a plausible explanation actively supported by both Plato, and far more recently by the work of Kieran Egan (2002). In other words, a child's present learning is derivative from past learning rather than stage development; a child must learn whole numbers, for example, before learning fractions. Egan (2002) explains:

> If, for example, one were to propose a theory that involved the claim that children would learn addition and subtraction before calculus, or would learn some sophisticated historical facts before developing a sophisticated historical consciousness, one would not be altogether surprised if empirical tests confirmed this part of one's theory. This confirmation would not be due to the claims being obvious psychological truths; rather it would be due to their logical necessity. (p. 29)

The empirical data collected through observation would be identical in such cases but the subsequent interpretation of the data would differ dramatically depending on whether an epistemological or psychological stage development lens was used to interpret the information.

This problem is further manifested in the aforementioned enduring conflict between student-centred and subject-centred pedagogical models. Proponents on both sides of the issue are able to present empirical research as "evidence" that supposedly supports their position. For example, Dianne Ravitch (2000) and E. D. Hirsch (2001) condemn child-centred learning practices that purportedly demonstrate progressive education as practically ineffective and highly romanticized in the tradition of Jean Jacques Rousseau's (1974) educational classic *Emile*. Alternatively, there is a plethora of teachers and researchers extolling the virtues of the child-centred practices found in progressive education practices and consistent with contemporary versions of constructivism that, for all intents and purposes, appear little different from the ideas associated with progressivism. How can both positions, supported by competing research findings, be correct?

Quite clearly, different conceptual lenses and normative commitments generate different research outcomes and ultimately lead to competing claims about what constitutes best practice. Once again, there is also the prevailing confusion in such research between empirical questions and philosophical ones, and the distinct kind of evidence required to answer questions in each respective category. This debate also illustrates how selective evidence is employed to advance one's particular ideological position. In this case, suffice to say that Hirsch and Ravitch who attack student-centred learning neglect to mention the Eight Year Study. This report is arguably the most comprehensive study ever conducted on the issue and provided compelling evidence on the academic effectiveness of student-centred approaches (Hyslop-Margison & Richardson, 2005; Hyslop-Margison & Sears, 2006).

In addition to the healthy scepticism regarding researcher objectivity that such cases ought to generate, these cases of conflicting conclusions once again illustrate the common confusion in education between empirical research and normative disagreement over what qualifies as a quality educational experience. If students are routinely drilled with propositional knowledge during their schooling years, they will undoubtedly acquire a greater acquisition of facts, or what Dewey (1916) described as "book learning," than students subjected to learner-centred approaches. Of course, the particular outcomes that emerge from each teaching style also create different learning outcomes and these outcomes are then evaluated on a subjective understanding of what qualifies as quality learning. Hence, the conceptual and analytic confusion is virtually unavoidable. Further, these are not matters to be settled by empirical study, but rather through philosophical debate. We will address the problematic nature of best practice claims in education in far greater detail in Chapter 5 when we demonstrate that many of the so-called research findings in this area are logical tautologies, or simply common sense.

Subject-centred learning in the form of lecture might be more effective for teaching students propositions about the world, or facts, while student-centred learning might be more effective in enhancing student interest, provoking class discussion, and generating the participatory dispositions consistent with active democratic citizenship. To complicate the matter even further, different students may respond differently to various types of instruction, and also to different types of instruction with different types of material. Teaching is, after all, a complex triadic relationship between the students, the teacher, and the subject matter. Each of these components contributes its own particular set of variables to each pedagogical context. Given these dynamics and the number of variables they generate, the conceptual contestations and the differing value commitments, it seems extremely outrageous from our perspective to suggest that a science of education is even a remote possibility.

4.7   The Direct Reference Theory of Language

In addition to the conceptual confusions and the problem of generalizability that undermine the validity of education research, there is also an implicit attachment to a Platonic or direct reference theory of meaning. Plato (1973) argued that ontological entities are provided with their conceptual meaning through a metaphysical attachment to the absolute perfect ontological form of the concept in question. A chair is a chair, then, because it partakes of the perfect form of chair. Somewhat derivative of this Platonic position is the *direct reference theory of meaning*, a theory of meaning that leads to fundamental misunderstandings about various educational concepts. Although the impact of this theory of meaning may initially seem relatively benign, the attending implications of extending the theory beyond its limited direct reference application generates deleterious ontological assumptions about words and what these words actually describe.

According to the direct reference theory of meaning, every word corresponds to some ontological entity or external object and nothing mediates between the word and the object in question. The fundamental assumption of the direct reference theory is that words are meaningful solely in virtue of having a denotation, i.e., the thing which the word or expression represents. There are many difficulties with this theory of language since it cannot account for quantifier phrases such as something, everything etc. or in situations such as Frege pointed out where the same denotation may have two different descriptive phrases. Frege's (1892) classic example, of course, is the *evening star* and the *morning star* that both refer to the planet Venus.

Gottlob Frege was a nineteenth-century mathematician, logician, and philosopher who arguably founded the analytic tradition in Western philosophy. The example of the evening star and morning star he thoughtfully employed clearly illustrated that the meaning of a symbol (or word) cannot be the object denoted as the direct reference theory suggests. Frege (1892) argued instead that meaning is determined by what he describes as the *sense* of the thing denoted. All objects, according to Frege, have senses that he defines as the various ways individuals think about the object in question, or the ways in which the object is presented. Sense, then, mediates between a sign and what the sign refers to rather than the sign directly referring to any object as suggested by the direct reference theory. This mediated theory of meaning cast serious dispersions on the direct reference theory of meaning, but, as we point out later, the latter's assumptions still implicitly seep their way deeply into educational discourse and research.

On the other hand, the direct reference theory of meaning is especially useful in explaining the connection between proper names and objects such as naming individuals. But as Wittgenstein (1963) effectively illustrated language simply does not operate in the logical positivist sense of words or concepts being neatly linked with objects or things in the world. Wittgenstein concisely described semantics – the way in which words "mean" – in the following way: "The meaning of a word is its use" (Wittgenstein, 1963, p. 56). Returning to the rather rough terrain of ordinary language to determine the meaning of words was far easier said than done, however, since the logical positivist movement had invested considerable energy into finding the perfectly descriptive language without any ambiguities or confusions.

Philosophical problems, including conceptual analysis, often run as deep as the forms of language and thought that set certain philosophers and education researchers on the road to various confusions. Wittgenstein (1963) correctly speaks of "illusions," "bewitchment," and "conjuring tricks" distorting our thinking through our forms of language, and he tries to free philosophy from their spell by attending to differences between superficially similar aspects of language that promote confusion. For much of the *Philosophical Investigations*, Wittgenstein (1963) illustrates how philosophers are led away from the world of ordinary language and the flexibility it entails by misleading aspects of language itself. These are where the pseudo-problems of philosophy are created, i.e., by misunderstanding how language beyond sign and reference functions.

Wittgenstein explored the role language plays in the development of various and specific philosophical problems, from some general problems involving language itself to some more specific problems in philosophy of mind. Throughout the *Philosophical Investigations*, the style of writing is conversational with Wittgenstein in turn playing the role of the befuddled philosopher (on either or both sides of traditional philosophical debates), and that of the guide attempting to show the philosopher the way back: the "way out of the fly bottle" (1963, p. 85). By helping educational researchers to understand the way ordinary language functions, they too can be shown the way out of the bottle.

We contend, then, that the bewitchment of language referred to by Wittgenstein continues to haunt education practice and education research. There is probably no better example than the concept of critical thinking where researchers in educational psychology still search for a concrete referent for a term that lacks any ontological status whatsoever. They pursue such practices as meta-analyses to determine an appropriate concept of critical thinking and how the practice might be pedagogically perfected.

More generally, researchers in education continue to treat terms such as critical thinking, creative thinking, imagination, citizenship, giftedness, intelligence, etc. as if such terms connected to particular ontological entities. A recent Social Sciences and Humanities Research Council grant, on which one of us played a collaborative philosophical role, illustrates that a search for some "correct" meaning of critical thinking continues by adopting as its primary mission the search to identify a correct "meaning" for critical thinking. It is like turning over a series of stones until finally the definitive definition of the concept is discovered. However, such a search is doomed to inevitable failure since mental process concepts, although having a meaning in the *sense* referred to by Frege and a meaning in ordinary language as argued by Wittgenstein, have no unique denotation.

We are not suggesting that sophisticated empirical researchers in education fail to appreciate that the terms and concepts they employ are strictly operational. What we are suggesting, however, is that empirical researchers in education speak, and act as if the concepts they apply actually enjoy some identifiable ontological status. These tacit assumptions lead to discursive misrepresentations of terms such as giftedness and critical thinking when the terms are used in educational classrooms or employed in discussions within teacher education programmes. The use of such language, cloaked in the outdated and limited direct reference theory of language, lends ontological credibility to concepts that they simply do not warrant. Critical thinking and giftedness are not part of the furniture of the world, but are educational constructs, and perhaps rather dubious ones at that.

Indeed, the discourse of giftedness provides an excellent case in point to illustrate this tacit commitment to direct reference theory. Although the concept, at best, may be operationally defined on the basis of administered tests, the following citation from a research-based textbook infers some actual ontological status upon the term:

> Giftedness occurs in 2 to 5 percent of school aged children. However, we do not yet understand what contributes most to giftedness, or why some gifted people achieve eminence and others fade into obscurity. The effects of heredity and environment are both important in the development of gifted and talented children, but the relative contribution of genetic and environmental factors is not clearly understood. (Winzer, 2001, p. 146)

There are a couple of serious problems, beyond the "not clearly understood" confession in the above passage that we believe are traceable to direct reference theory assumptions. First, to talk about giftedness, a normative concept determined by a social, cultural, and educational preference for certain abilities, as a biological characteristic bestowed on individuals through genetics incorrectly places giftedness in the same category as hair color, muscular dystrophy, or other genetically determined characteristics and diseases. Muscular dystrophy is certainly not a social construct, but giftedness clearly is a social construct.

Within the quoted passage we offer above, it is also important to note the normative language that divides gifted individuals into the simplistic categories of "eminence" or "obscurity" with a clear inference that eminence, whatever that entails, is the appropriate domain for this group of individuals. According to this assumption, all intelligent people ought to be successful as defined by some rather narrow cultural presuppositions about what defines success. There is little to no consideration given to the possibility that many so-called gifted individuals may simply choose obscurity as a personal preference over some other high-profile life style. Clearly, obscurity is not in itself a definitive sign of abject failure and even more clearly the associated claim is not an empirical one.

We have attempted to illustrate in this last section that although direct reference theory is very narrow in its proper application, i.e., it is basically restricted to proper names, its implications still very much influence the way educators and researchers discuss, analyse, and employ various concepts. It is therefore critically important that researchers in education cease searching for the definitive or Platonic meanings of these terms and understand that their usage is simply a function, sometimes a confused one, of educational discourse. As such, the concepts have no ontological status beyond their use in ordinary language and a search for ultimate meaning of terms such as critical thinking simply puts Wittgenstein's fly back in the bottle.

4.8 Summary

The scientific study of human beings is obviously beset with a range of problems that ignore conceptual confusions, normative intrusions into data interpretations and in general undermine the existential ideals of human self-determination. Students are not objects that can be observed, and objectively reported on, nor can axiomatic pedagogical principles be subsequently identified. The threat to student well-being posed by such objectification is most manifest in the process of labeling that occurs far too frequently among educational psychologists as they identify certain members of the population as belonging to pseudo-categories that often do far more damage than good.

Indeed, the ethical values that form the basis of successful human interaction are viewed as an impediment to work in the social sciences and we must ultimately confront the question of whether empirical research on students violates their human subjectivity and ignores their basic capacity for agency. It is in light of such troubling observations that perhaps we ought to heed ever more closely poet W. H. Auden's purported satiric commandment about social research activities in general when he stated: "Thou shall not sit with statisticians or commit a social science."

Chapter 5
Education Research as Analytic Truths

The Pseudo-Empirical Claims of Empirical Study

5.1 Introduction

As we have pointed out in Chapters 1–4, there are continued concerted contemporary efforts to promote empirically based research in education to the almost complete exclusion of other research paradigms. In the USA, these efforts are most notably illustrated "in the No Child Left Behind Act, and the reauthorization and reorganization of the Office of Educational Research and Improvement as the Institute for Educational Science" (Maxwell, 2004, p. 3). The Bush administration's No Child Left Behind (NCLB) legislation considers scientific research the best available means to improve education, supporting only those studies that, "employ systematic, empirical methods that draw on observation and experiment" (NCLB, 2000). As we have pointed out, this position is further instantiated by both the National Research Council in the USA and the Social Sciences and Humanities Research Council of Canada.

The increased emphasis on social science research methods and on educational psychology within faculties and departments of education further indicates a growing confidence in the ability of empirical research to strengthen classroom practices. In this chapter, we wish to supply additional evidence that this confidence in empirical research to resolve education problems is woefully misplaced.

In this chapter, and in stark contrast to the prevailing perspective described above, we adopt A. R. Louch's (1966), Jan Smedslund's (1979), and Kieran Egan's (2002) critical framework that correctly suggests: "A great deal of the empirical research in education involves the confusion of trying to establish empirical connections between things that are already conceptually tied" (p. 166). In addition to elucidating Egan's position in particular on the problem, we apply his analytical framework to assess the actual contribution to classroom practice of empirical research on contemporary citizenship education conducted by two major international organizations: the International Association for the Evaluation of Educational Achievement (IEA) and the National Foundation for Educational Research (NFER). By examining these studies through the lens that Egan provides, we evaluate whether their recommendations for classroom practice are simply definitions, or restatements, of what we mean in a normative and ordinary language sense by the concept of democratic citizenship. We conclude in this chapter that there is, in fact, a persistent pattern of analytic connections between the concept of democratic citizenship and the pedagogical recommendations offered by these two highly respected (and extremely expensive) studies. We will also discuss the idea of so-called best practice, the holy grail of educational research, and consider why the search for same is doomed to failure as predicted by Egan's critique.

The analysis we provide in this chapter, and in the other chapters for that matter, will certainly not eliminate empirical research in education – indeed that is not entirely our objective – but general awareness of the problems we discuss may reduce the tremendous human and financial resource expenditures on fundamentally flawed research practices that do not and cannot deliver on their promise of strengthening teaching and learning. Again, our genuine hope is that these funds will be directed toward more fruitful forms of education expenditures that grapple with issues of serious social inequality, higher salaries for qualified teachers, and investigating the moral and civic responsibilities of schools in democratic societies.

In Section 5.2, we briefly review some general problems with empirical research in education as a prelude to explaining Egan's critical framework. We also offer some initial examples of educational research where the recommendations for classroom practice are quite clearly analytically connected to the studied concept to help elucidate the problem Egan identifies. In Section 5.3, we review the two citizenship education studies selected for analysis and evaluate their respective recommendations for classroom practice. In Section 5.4, we illustrate that any contributions empirical research might make in identifying appropriate teaching methods are exceptionally limited in nature and most frequently fall victim to the critique Egan advances. We conclude the chapter by briefly considering the implications of our findings for empirical research in education more generally.

5.2   Conceptual Confusion and Logical Tautology

There are, as we have pointed out throughout this text, numerous and well-documented difficulties with applying scientific principles to explaining or understanding the complicated dynamics of human behaviour. We will not rehearse these arguments here since we have already dealt with them at considerable length elsewhere in these pages but it is worthwhile to reiterate a couple of the most salient criticisms of human science research practices relevant to the critique we advance in this chapter.

One trenchant criticism of applying empirical methods to the study of humans contrasts the numerous successes of the natural sciences against those noticeably absent in the social sciences (Miller, 1991). This criticism is especially true in education where advocates of empirical approaches, particularly in the area of educational psychology, are hard pressed to identify any meaningful contribution that their research has provided to improve classroom practice (Egan, 2002; Levin, 2003).

No overarching predictive or explanatory learning theories in education have remotely achieved the scientific status of general relativity, DNA theory, or evolutionary biology, and there is widespread disagreement among researchers regarding the accuracy of many long-standing educational theories such as developmental learning (Egan, 2002). Other criticisms of the social sciences point out their susceptibility to the ideological commitments of researchers and to the sheer dynamic complexity of human behaviour (Aronowitz, 1988; Gould, 1996). Some critics have even suggested that searching for a systematic explanation of human, social, and educational phenomena is simply a misguided endeavour condemned to the failure it has heretofore experienced because it fails to account for human agency (Barrow, 1981; Miller, 1991).

One prevalent problem with empirical research in education that is largely ignored arises from researchers' disregard for the value judgements that inevitably occur during their analysis of collected data. Indeed, we have discussed this issue in some detail in the previous four chapters. Egan (2002) highlights the persistent problem of value judgements in the social sciences specifically as they relate to education research by suggesting the conflation of fact with value, the cardinal sin Weber warns researchers against, is virtually unavoidable given the contestable nature of the investigated concepts in the field, including, as we demonstrate later in this chapter, the concept of democratic citizenship.

As Egan (2002) suggests, the established goals in education are inevitably normative and must be identified through moral debate and/or philosophical analysis rather than through empirical study. For example, a concept such as *democratic citizenship* is connected to a range of supporting normative ideas, judgements, and behaviours that have direct pedagogical implications. The ideas, judgements, and behaviours we connect to the concept of citizenship bear directly on the type of classroom practices we will subsequently advocate. The teaching of democratic citizenship, then, is antecedently bound up with the particular normative concept of democratic citizenship that we adopt. The teaching of any specific quality is logically connected with our conceptual analysis of the concept in question and our interpretation of "quality" a consequence of that relationship. The appropriate forms of instruction, in other words, follow from the qualities of a democratic citizen and do not require empirical study to determine their practical pedagogical implications.

In *Getting It Wrong From The Beginning: Our Progressivist Inheritance From Herbert Spencer, John Dewey and Jean Piaget*, Egan (2002) observes that most empirical research conducted in education has had "no discernible impact on general educational achievement" (p. 151). He dismisses the range of standard responses typically advanced by researchers to explain the problem (see, e.g. Levin, 2003) such as inadequate teacher education, teacher inattention to research findings, poor communication of results, or the need for additional research in the area under investigation.

On Egan's account, the problems of educational research are much more fundamental. He argues that the recommendations for classroom practice offered by the majority of empirical research in education simply advance definitions of the investigated concept as recommendations for classroom practice. In other words, the studied concept, in this particular case *democratic citizenship*, is analytically linked to the subsequent pedagogical recommendations antecedent to any empirically discovered relationship. The statement that "all bachelors are unmarried men," where the predicate (unmarried men) is contained in the subject (bachelors), offers a classic example of an analytic proposition, or logical tautology. An analysis of the concept of bachelor reveals a logical necessity in the above proposition because all individuals fitting that classification are, by definition, unmarried men.

Egan also employs the critique of psychology advanced by Ludwig Wittgenstein to highlight the problem in applying empirical methods derived from science to education research. In *Philosophical Investigations*, Wittgenstein (1963) observes that:

> The confusion and bareness of psychology is not to be explained by calling it a young science; its state is not comparable with physics, for instance, in its beginnings. For in psychology there are experimental methods and conceptual confusion. The existence of the experimental method makes us think we have the means of solving the problems which trouble us; though problem and method pass one another by. (p. 232)

Wittgenstein suggests, then, that psychology is not simply a young science struggling to establish an epistemic foundation and suitable methodology such as the case with a developing science like physics. The confusion in psychology is the result of a more fundamental rupture between the problems it studies and the method it applies to address these problems. In other words, the confusion is caused by applying the experimental method borrowed from science to evaluate human behaviour against a set of non-empirical normative concepts – many of which are subject to the conceptual errors and problematic assumptions we have described in previous chapters.

Egan admits that his criticism of empirical research in education is not entirely original, but rather is indebted to an earlier analysis of social science research by Norwegian Jan Smedslund. The latter published an article in 1979 in the *Scandinavian Journal of Psychology* entitled "Between the analytic and the arbitrary: A case of psychological research." Smedslund argues that the empirical generalizations emerging from social science research actually explicate the analytical relationship "between ordinary language concepts" (p. 129). He analyses a range of social science research claims in the article to illustrate their pseudo-empirical nature and draws the following conclusion:

> The theoretical analysis contains elements of both the analytic and arbitrary, but neither is overtly acknowledged. The analytic element is incompatible with the aspiration to empirical testing and the arbitrary element is incompatible with the aspiration to generality and timelessness. These latent contradictions can remain generally undiscovered only as long as the standards for theoretical precision remain at their current low level. Meanwhile, the façade of scientific respectability is only maintained by the advanced technology for data gathering and analysis. (p. 140)

According to Smedslund, then, the problem – largely masked behind a deceiving and distracting smokescreen of complex scientific methodology and statistical sophistication – is twofold. The truly empirical findings of social science research are arbitrary, or non-generalizable, while the generalizable propositions are simply logical necessities.

Even previous to Smedslund's somewhat damning and largely ignored critique of social science, Egan points out that A. R. Louch (1966) had challenged Edward Thorndike's "law of effect" on similar grounds. Thondike claimed to have "discovered" the scientific principle that people repeat behaviours when such actions have pleasurable consequences. In response to this rather unspectacular claim, Louch argued that in fact the relationship between repeated behaviours and pleasurable consequences is conceptually linked and, hence, Thorndike's claim is pseudo-empirical. In other words, repeat behaviour is logically or analytically connected to the concept of pleasure.

It may help to elucidate the problem Egan identifies through a more immediate hypothetical example related to citizenship education, the subject area we target for analysis later in this chapter. Suppose researchers choose to investigate whether students who participate in community-based programmes possess a stronger sense of civic responsibility than students who are not involved in such activities. A classical experimental design such as that advocated by NCLB and the NRC is employed that involves a carefully selected control group and an experimental group. Following a series of longitudinal studies, surveys, observations, questionnaires, and interviews, the researchers conclude that the experimental group demonstrates a statistically significant increase in civic engagement over the control group. But what have we actually learned as a result of this supposedly empirical investigation? Following Egan, we seriously question whether such claims constitute genuine empirical findings since the concepts of civic engagement and community involvement are analytically related. To put the point even more simply, community involvement is correlated with civic engagement because community involvement is the conceptual equivalent of civic engagement.

The How People Learn project in the USA offers an actual example of education research that further illustrates Egan's point. National Research Council researchers, both well funded and supposedly extremely qualified in the field of education, sought a scientific research base to identify the best available classroom practices. After a series of studies and the employment of elaborate research and data analysis methods, their recommendations for best practice include the following surprisingly banal observations: "To develop competence in an area of inquiry, students must (a) have a deep foundation of factual knowledge, (b) understand facts and ideas in the context of a conceptual framework, and (c) organize knowledge in ways that facilitate retrieval and application" (Donovan et al., 1999, p. 12). As Egan (2002) correctly points out, the principles of effective learning identified in this report are simply normative appraisals, or definitions, of competence within a particular area of inquiry. Our own investigation of a related section from the same study reveals additional conceptual linkages in the various empirical research outcomes and claims for pedagogical practice:

> In-depth understanding requires detailed knowledge of the facts within a domain. The key attribute of expertise is a detailed and organized understanding of the important facts within a specific domain. Education needs to provide children with sufficient mastery of

the details of particular subject matters so that they have a foundation for further exploration
within those domains. (Donovan et al., 1999, p. 11)

Once again, the conclusions reached and recommendations for classroom practice
are analytically connected to the researched concepts. For example, "expertise"
may be normatively defined as "a detailed and organized understanding of the
important facts within a particular domain," and we obviously do not require
massively funded research schemes to demonstrate empirically the analytic
relationship between subject mastery and domain expertise.

Egan dutifully notes that a number of research practices are, at least on the face
of it, less vulnerable to this particular line of criticism. Some qualitative and
phenomenological research practices in education appear more or less immune to
this critique since their claims are often admittedly contextual in nature. Another
form of empirical research that evades Egan's criticism includes those studies focused
on counting things such as the number of times boys are called on in classrooms
as opposed to girls (see, e.g. Sadker & Sadker, 1995).

However, claims emerging from these types of studies may be specific to the
observed situation and, hence, potentially fall into the arbitrary category previously
identified by Smedslund. For example, when such findings vary between classrooms and between schools, they become, "arbitrary elements, which are genuinely
empirical, [but] cannot be generalized" (Egan, 2002, p. 169). Further, when the
implications for classroom practice are considered from studies such as those
described earlier, a point Egan unfortunately neglects to consider, we once again
end up with simple analytic imperatives such as "gender equality requires treating
boys and girls the same in classrooms." The implication of this research for classroom practice might be stated in the following conditional statement: If we want to
create equal academic opportunities for boys and girls, then both sexes must enjoy
equal classroom experiences – or if A then A, another particularly blatant logical
tautology.

5.3   The Case of Citizenship Education

The two studies we selected for investigation in this chapter were chosen on the
basis of their high international profile, the respect the participating researchers
have garnered within the field of citizenship education, and the broad significant
funding the research received from a wide range of stakeholders. In their respective
reports, both of these studies provide a lengthy and detailed discussion of their
methods and their eventual research findings. Consistent with the critical framework we adopt, our analysis in this chapter focuses entirely on their recommendations for classroom practice. It is also worth mentioning that we sought expert
external guidance in selecting these studies for investigation by requesting a full
professor with an international reputation in the field to identify two highly
regarded studies in citizenship education. We specifically requested that he select
studies that he believed were immune to Egan's critique. Hence, we wish to emphasize

categorically that these studies were not self-selected for their predetermined vulnerability to our forthcoming analysis. They do, however, as we shall demonstrate, fall victim to that analysis in a very prototypical fashion.

The International Association for the Evaluation of Educational Achievement's (IEA) web page states that, "The IEA (2005) Civic Education Study is the largest and most rigorous study of civic education ever conducted internationally." The scope of this study is indicated by the fact that researchers tested and surveyed more than 90,000 14-year-old students in 28 countries, and 50,000 17–19-year-old students in 16 countries between 1999 and 2000. The IEA reports that teachers and principals also participated in the study by offering insights and participating in interviews. The research instrument selected for the study measured knowledge and attitudes toward democracy, national identity, social cohesion, and diversity. The level of youth engagement in civil society was also a central focus of this large-scale and well-respected international investigation.

The IEA Civic Education Study was a broadly funded research and cooperative enterprise involving the IEA (its Headquarters in Amsterdam and national research institutes in the participating countries), the Humboldt University of Berlin (the International Coordinating Center), and the International Steering Committee. The Center for Civic Education Study in the Department of Human Development at the University of Maryland at College Park has financially and academically supported the work of the International Steering Committee for IEA and its Chair since 1994. According to the organization: "Its continuing mission is to promote the dissemination of findings and advance research on civic knowledge and engagement based on the study" (IEA, 2005). Hence, as we mentioned earlier, it is a research venture that enjoyed considerably broad and substantial funding, and drew on significant academic and research expertise. The credentials accumulated by both the organization and individuals involved in this study are exceptionally high on all possible fronts, a fact that makes the upcoming analysis of its findings that much more troubling.

One module of the research instrument employed by the IEA prepared a series of case studies to identify the most effective practices in civic education programmes. The subsequent analysis of these case studies revealed general agreement among experts in citizenship education and includes the following suggestions: "Civics education courses should be participative, interactive, related to life in school and community, conducted in a non-authoritarian environment, and cognizant of diversity" (Amadeo et al., 2002, p. 23). However, an analysis of these identified best practices in civics education lends additional credence to Egan's contention that empirical research in education simply advances analytic propositions in its recommendations for practice. Quite clearly, participation, interaction, non-authoritarian relationships with community and an awareness of diversity are fundamental characteristics of democratic citizenship. The best practices identified by these case studies are anterior to the conducted research, and simply represent analytic connections between a generally accepted concept of citizenship and recommendations for civics education. There is nothing empirically revealed in this research and the claims for best practice in citizenship education are simply definitions of democratic citizenship.

In the final analysis and despite its employment of relatively complex statistical instruments and research methods, the lengthy IEA study we investigated offers surprisingly little discussion of its actual implications for classroom practice beyond the previously cited recommendations. However, in the closing pages of the report the researchers finally ask and respond to the following question: "In short, what have we learned from the IEA Civic Education Study?" (Amadeo et al., 2002, p. 171). The responses provided by the researchers only serve to reconfirm the analytic nature of their recommendations, and provide additional and compelling warrant for Egan's critique:

> We can see civic knowledge is important, but not enough. Tolerance, willingness to participate, and understanding responsibilities as well as rights are important elements of citizenship in democracies. While there is no single approach that is likely to enhance all facets of citizenship, the school can play a valuable role. School factors predicted civic knowledge and engagement for both the lower and upper secondary school students. It would seem that schools offer places for students to practice democracy as much as they offer places for learning facts. (Amadeo et al., 2002, p. 171)

Extensive and resource draining empirical research is not required to establish that tolerance, willingness to participate, and understanding responsibilities as well as rights are important and required elements of democratic citizenship. These various qualities would be included in any comprehensive conceptual analysis of democratic citizenship. Indeed, the concepts of tolerance, willingness to participate, and understanding rights and responsibilities are inextricably connected to what we mean by democratic citizenship. The observation that democracy should be practiced in classrooms and schools as well as taught arguably represents another analytic claim. Dewey (1916), for example, established the relationship between dispositions, political engagement, and classroom practice in the absence of any empirical research almost a century ago. Hence, not only are the claims of this extraordinarily expensive and resource draining study analytic in nature, they are almost a century old.

The National Foundation for Educational Research (NFER) has been working since 1946 as a British-based organization to provide various stakeholders with practical research and responsive assessment programmes designed to promote "excellence in education and lifelong learning" (2005). According to the NFER, it aims to "improve education and training, nationally and internationally, by undertaking research, development and dissemination activities and by providing information services. The NFER undertakes approximately 200 research projects every year and its work spans all areas and age groups in education" (NFER, 2005).

The NFER research article we selected for analysis in this chapter is entitled *Taking Post-16 Citizenship Forward: Learning from the Post-16 Citizenship Development Projects*. Once again, we reiterate the study was not self-selected, but was instead chosen by a recognized expert in the field based on its purported immunity to the challenge we advance. The report's recommendations for classroom practice are based on "interviews with 67 individuals and 26 groups of young people across 20 case study organizations" (Craig et al., 2004, p. 6). The study evaluates a series of pilot projects that were undertaken in September 2001 designed to identify the best available methods, or best practices, to deliver citizenship education to students between the ages of 14–19. The initial 3-year project ended with a final round of pilot projects in 2003. The entire study involved some 79 different organizations around the world concerned with citizenship education. Similar to the IEA, then, the NFER investigation is an extremely well-funded, well-respected and influential research study within the field of citizenship education.

The NFER (Craig et al., 2004) study offers a series of observations in its executive summary that supposedly underlie effective post-16 citizenship education including: "An emphasis on combining knowledge, understanding and skills with practical action – what is termed a political literacy in action approach, as opposed to a narrower political knowledge approach (p. 6)," and "Involvement and participation of young people in decisions about learning, and the development of a student voice" (p. 7). Once again, a disconcerting pattern of analytic connections between the concept of democratic citizenship and the subsequent recommendations for classroom practice is readily apparent in the conclusions reached by NFER researchers.

A meaningful construct of democratic citizenship necessarily entails the practical application of political knowledge, understanding, and skills. Someone who was not politically engaged in this practical sense, either formally or informally, would not be considered a democratic citizen in the fullest sense of the term. Further, the NFER claim that the development of student voice is a necessary condition of future political engagement simply reiterates the IEA finding on the importance of democratic classroom practice and, hence, remains subject to precisely the same criticism we outlined earlier. As we pointed out, Dewey understood this connection as logically necessary rather than empirical a full century ago.

The executive summary of the NFER report also includes a list of what it describes as successful approaches to citizenship education. The list includes the following recommendations for classroom practice in citizenship education: (1) negotiation of key issues of interest with young people; (2) development of a critically reflective environment, with scope for discussion and debate; (3) facilitation of activities based on the active involvement of young people rather than the teaching of knowledge, understanding and skills; and (4) involving young people in active participation in large-scale assemblies such as student parliaments (Craig et al, 2004, p. v). Simply by extracting some of the key concepts in these recommendations their definitional quality, or analyticity, is manifestly apparent. For example, the use of negotiation to resolve key issues, rather than imposing arbitrary settlements, is a fundamental democratic practice and accepting this process is a requirement of the generally accepted concept of democratic citizenship. Similarly, a critically reflective environment that fosters the active involvement and participation of individuals in a formal parliamentary, or even more informal, format is a necessary condition of meaningful democratic citizenship.

The two studies we have reviewed in this section underscore the importance of Louch's (1966), Smedlund's (1979), and Egan's (2002) charge that so-called empirical findings in social science generally, and education more specifically, are little more than analytic claims following logically from the concept under investigation.

In Section 5.5, we continue to apply this critical framework against some of the major claims related to what commonly qualifies as "best practice" as identified by empirical research in teaching and learning.

5.4 Empirical Research and Teaching Methods

We believe the search for axiological principles that can be applied to teaching in an attempt to ensure successful learning is misguided on a variety of levels. We have already outlined in previous chapters the complex range of variables that influence any classroom context, the potential impact of student agency on learning outcomes, the fact that different subject matter calls for different instructional approaches, and how teachers' personalities are themselves key factors in achieving pedagogical success. In this section we will elaborate on some of these points and raise other issues that illustrate the limitations of empirical research in developing quality instruction or identifying what are commonly referred to as "best practices."

Barrow (1981) makes the critically important point that empirical research in education can never be scientific in any meaningful sense of the term when it comes to identifying axiological pedagogical principles. It is worth quoting Barrow at some length on this point about teaching methods as he cites an unpublished manuscript by Ruth Barwood to reinforce his contention that such a search is inevitably fruitless:

> Looking at what happens in classrooms is not analogous to looking at what happens in test tubes, and to suggest that we should proceed as if it were, since science is the norm of our thinking, is to radically misunderstand science. Science is the study of matter, and matter is all that test tubes contain. Classrooms also contain minds. When molecules collide, they do not do so either unintentionally or deliberately, they simply collide. When people interact, they do not simply interact, there is meaning in their interaction. If we ask why molecules collide we are asking for reasons that are causal. If we ask why a particular human action took place, some but not all of the reasons asked for will be causal. If we observe a child's arm rise in a classroom, a scientific explanation for this can be offered in terms of electrical impulses in the brain. This is an explanation of how and why his arm raises. To understand why he raises his arm we can only speculate about shared social conventions and their application to this particular incident. Any description or explanation of an action that fails to take account of its purpose is an incomplete description: to suppose otherwise is to overlook the fundamental difference between actions and happenings, between people and things. (p. 180)

The critical point here, of course, is that human intentions within particular contexts inevitably influence action both in the world and, more specifically, within classrooms. Any generalizations that emerge from classroom observations are therefore unable to provide a full account of such reasons and, hence, the complete understanding of causality is impossible. Without achieving such an understanding of the causes behind student behaviour, the hope of identifying axiological teaching principles is little more than a chimera.

There are, of course, as we have argued throughout the previous chapters, any number of factors that are beyond empirical study and yet impact forcefully on teaching and learning outcomes. Barrow (1981) cites a number of variables that are often not controlled for in classroom experiments and yet profoundly influence the context of both the individual learner and the classroom in question and, hence, whatever learning may or may not occur. For example, these forces include the attitudes of parents, differences in social class, different qualities and characteristics of schools, different reactions of children to the fact they are being tested and differences in the quality, experience, and personality of the teachers involved to name only a few. Clearly, some modern statistical methods claim the ability to be able to control for a range of variables, but since this range is virtually infinite in nature, we contend that such statistical claims are more misleading than they are convincing.

What is typically missing in any empirical account of what matters in good teaching is its relationship to the sensitive handling of human relationships. Good teachers make effective use of their particularly personalities that, of course, differ dramatically in character from one teacher to the next. If we simply recall our own education there are no doubt memories of different teachers who employed radically different approaches, but were nonetheless successful (and many who were not) in conveying their message to students. There is not a single path to good teaching, but many different paths depending on what any given teacher might bring to the teaching enterprise. Part of what promotes good teaching is clearly understanding one's personal strengths and weaknesses in this regard and trying to utilize one's strengths and minimize one's weaknesses. This understanding makes the very idea of "best practice" more than technically problematic since it is professionally unethical and even dangerous to coerce some teachers into using methods they are simply not comfortable employing.

Perhaps one of the most contemporary and dangerous examples of the idea that quality teaching can be quantified is expressed through the use of questionnaires to "measure" teaching quality. Barrow (1981) describes some of the questions that are typically asked on university questionnaires that are designed to measure the effectiveness of faculty instruction: Is this course relevant? Does the instructor know his material? Does he easily build rapport with his class? Does he make learning more interesting than you expected? Have you made progress through the course? Are students in this class interested in getting to know one another? As Barrow points out, faculty members' jobs literally depend on the answers students provide to these and other similar inane and potentially irrelevant questions, questions that are not only flawed in design but overly presumptuous about what questions students are qualified to answer.

For example, it is highly questionable to assume that students are positioned to know whether the course or the material it contains is relevant (e.g. relevant to what or to whom, one might ask) or that students are able to judge effectively the knowledge and expertise of a professor about a subject matter they presumably know very little if anything at all about. It is worth pointing out that all of the earlier examples are taken directly from actual course questionnaires. Second, there is also the question of objectivity since studies on course evaluations clearly indicate scores awarded by students are skewed by issues such as instructor personality, instructor appearance, whether or not the course is compulsory and, most notably, the grades students are receiving in the course from the professor involved. There is much discussion and concern about grade inflation in contemporary university settings, but little incentive to remove the major force driving student grades skyward. Why might this be the case?

In spite of their obvious lack of validity, i.e., they simply do not assess what they target, student course evaluations represent a central administrative strategy ideologically designed to maintain institutional control over faculty, especially those faculty who resist increasing measures of institutional control over their work, assessment practices, and course content. These evaluations operationally define good teaching by equating it with statistically high scores awarded by students.

The view that course evaluations, based on the problematic assumptions about learning, teaching, and education we outlined earlier, provide a useful measure of teaching excellence offers an excellent example and lucid illustration of Foucault's (1991) postulate on the relationship between truth and power. The inferred quality of a given faculty member's teaching, in this case the aggregate scores and abstracted narrative comments on course evaluation forms, is linked in a circular relationship with a system of power, i.e., the university's promotion and tenure process. The regime that defines truth is precisely the same administrative body that achieves institutional control over a specified population on the basis of that definition. Course evaluations are also illustrative of Foucault's concern on the panoptic supervision of all social beings since the teachers report on the students and the students are compelled to report on teachers. In a very real sense, all of the players are being watched without the aid of classroom cameras.

The absurdity of course evaluations conducted by students is really quite obvious since such measures, quantified or otherwise, lack any meaningful validity related to actual teacher competence. Of course, an effective analysis of teaching, if such an analysis is even possible, is far more complicated than any simple quantified system based on scores awarded by students might realistically capture. Such an analysis would begin with a coherent conception of what constitutes teaching excellence and quality education, including specified aims, objectives, and practices that include specific content knowledge. The practices of teachers would then be assessed against these established principles and student content acquisition. However, since we lack the former, the latter is impossible and any attempt to identify best practice will be founded on a particular set of assumptions rather than on any amount of specific student learning.

Once again, empirical methods and scientism, in this case statistical data, are conflated with normative questions and the conclusions subsequently drawn are woefully invalid. Nevertheless, in their present form course evaluations provide the university with an important mechanism of institutional control cloaked in validity to punish faculty for deviant political behaviour when deemed necessary by conservative ideological forces. Consistent with the consumer approach to higher education, student course evaluations also reveal the level of customer satisfaction with a particular faculty member, a far more important consideration in the contemporary market-driven university milieu than the actual quality of education.

Sanders (1978) published an important article, "Teacher effectiveness: Accepting the null hypothesis," in which he challenges behaviourist analyses of teacher effectiveness. His argument strikes to the core against current empirical research assumptions that there is an inevitable or detectable relationship between specific pedagogical approaches and actual classroom learning. The entire idea that tinkering with classroom practice will enhance student learning is tacitly founded on the rather vulgar simplicity of a stimulus-response, or behaviourist, pedagogical model. Within this framework, there is the corresponding implication that, "there should be a consistent empirical relationship between quantitative and/or qualitative differences in teacher behavior and levels of student achievement outcomes" (p. 184). This assumption not only supports the current plethora of empirical testing and NRC funding practices but the current micro-level accountability measures embraced by NCLB in the USA.

Sanders (1978) points out that the behaviourist view rests on the assumption that teacher effectiveness is entirely determined by increased measures of student learning, or as he puts the matter: "The proof of teacher effective lies in the pudding of student achievement" (p. 185). In order for this particular thesis to hold true, he suggest that all other variables must be controlled for or held constant, a serious problem considering the fluidity and dynamics of human behaviour that we have described throughout this text. Although his examples are extreme and perhaps even somewhat crude, they make the point in question very effectively:

> It would obviously make little sense to judge a teacher of the mentally retarded as less effective than a teacher of gifted children because the former failed to produce comparable levels of reading achievement in his students. Clearly, ability differences account for much, if not most, of the variance in reading achievement between the two groups of students. Strictly speaking, then, the empirical meaning of teacher effectiveness, and thus accountability, depends upon a *ceteris paribus* clause with respect to all other plausible determinants of student achievement. (Sanders, 1978, p. 185)

On this basis, Sanders not only questions the tenability of empirical research into teaching and learning but states without equivocation that teacher behaviour is not differentially related to student outcomes. In other words, to infer that student learning is a direct function of teacher performance misunderstands the causal relationship between the two behaviours. He proceeds to cite one of the most comprehensive reviews of the period on empirical research into teaching that clearly indicates any evidence supporting the relationship between teaching behaviour and student learning is entirely lacking.

Sanders quotes from a book entitled *Teachers Make a Difference* that reluctantly reached the following conclusion after a comprehensive study of the relationship between teaching and learning: "We would like to suggest how teachers make a difference. Unfortunately, research has not yet linked teacher behavior with student achievement in a direct associative way. Thus it is impossible to say that teaching behaviors x, y, and z are associated with distinct areas of student achievement" (Sanders, 1978, p. 185). And the truth is that we are still waiting for such evidence to present itself today. Instead, the evidence, at least for those willing to seriously examine it, continues to lead us in the other direction by suggesting empirical research in education has produced virtually no reliable or valid connections between specified teaching practices and student learning outcomes.

Another compelling report supporting Sanders' (1978) null hypothesis is the so-called Coleman Report. This report concluded that differences in school quality, or private versus public schools, failed to account for much if any of the variance in student achievement beyond what was already predictable based on student academic ability and socio-economic status. Sanders argues that if these types of backgrounds were genuinely controlled for in the course of empirical research, then any effects related entirely to school and teaching differences would virtually disappear. The 1966 Coleman report was cited by school districts around the country as evidence that integrating African-American children into white schools would have little or no effect on student achievement. As a result of his findings, Coleman was in high demand as an expert witness for the school districts that argued against the busing of students from poor urban areas into more rural and affluent areas. It is also important to note that the 1966 Coleman report explained differences in academic achievement between whites and blacks as a by-product of a culture of poverty rather than the quality of teaching or schools they attended. This culture of poverty had a greater influence on African-Americans because of a higher concentration of poverty among this ethnic group.

We have used the work of Louch (1966) at several times in this text to support our claim that empirical research in education is a profoundly flawed enterprise. Fenstermacher (1979) also quotes Louch's philosophical critique by citing him on the point we raised previously in this chapter: "Triviality, redundancy, and tautology are the epithets which I think can be properly applied to the behaviorist scientist" (cited in Fenstermacher, 1979, p. 157). The persistence of education research, however, according to Fenstermacher involves the lack of attention researchers pay to the actual problems raised by philosophers challenging their enterprise. Fenstermacher describes the problem this way:

> Many education researchers, when they seek assistance from philosophy, look to philosophy of science for guidance on such matters as the nature of evidence, the logic of explanation and proof, the conceptual features of causation and probability, and criteria for hypothesis and theory construction. Though the value of philosophy of science to educational research may be great, it provides little assistance on how to think about the phenomenon of education. That is, philosophy of science may be a boon to the improvement of educational research, but it is not likely to add much at all to our understanding of what it means to do research in education. (p. 156)

Fenstermacher is making a similar point to the one that we have raised throughout the course of our discussion. Although research theories may create a more sophisticated approach to empirical research in education, they do not address what constitutes a rationally justified and morally defensible model of schooling or education. Hence, the idea of making progress in education from empirical analysis and statistical methods is fundamentally and scientifically misguided.

5.5   The Analytic Nature of Best Practice Claims

As we have mentioned previously, the search for so-called best practices in teaching drives most empirical research in education. This search has its unfortunate underpinnings in the work of Herbert Spencer and his pseudoscientific principles that we discussed via Kieran Egan in a previous chapter and continues undaunted today as a literal army of empirical researchers and their camp followers in contemporary education continue the fruitless march. In this section, we explore claims of best practice as identified by Joseph Codde (2007) in his online version of work adapted from Arthur W. Chickering's and Zelda F. Gamson's (1991) book entitled *Seven Principles for Good Practice in Undergraduate Education* and David Pratt's (1994) identification of best practices in *Curriculum Planning: A Handbook for Professionals*. We will illustrate in the following discussion that these so-called best practices amount to nothing more than analytic rather than empirical claims.

The first principle of good teaching practice cited by Codde suggests that "good practice encourages student-faculty contact." Codde adds that he makes every attempt to ensure his students attend class regularly, know his students by name, and serves as a mentor and informal advisor to his students. Quite obviously, no amount of empirical research is required to reveal these practices are consistent with positive outcomes related to teaching. Students who do not attend class, on the whole, are bound to do much more poorly academically than those students who attend class, listen to lectures, take notes, or participate in other class activities. Further, students who develop a personal kinship with an instructor who in turn knows their name and something about them will be far more apt to engage the content of that particular class. Caring about one's students and the subject matter one teaches is logically antecedent to creating an effective classroom environment. None of these claims require empirical research since, for example, attending class is simply a necessary condition of learning in class and the two activities are analytically connected in advance of empirical study.

Another claim advanced by Codde based on "empirical research" is a classic favourite cited in many teacher education textbooks and that is: "Good practice emphasizes time on task." This particular "principle" of "good practice" is almost so obviously analytical that it requires virtually no explanation beyond its self-explanatory relationship. Why would empirical research be necessary to reveal that students who spend more time working academically will be more successful than students who choose to fritter away their time at something else? Quite clearly, time on task and learning are inherently interconnected because the concepts in question are pedagogically linked.

One final example – although we could cite more – drawn from Codde's seven principles for good practice in education cites the importance of communicating high expectations. Underneath this more general claim, Codde's principle includes some of the following imperatives:

- I encourage students to excel at the work they do.
- I encourage students to work hard in class.

- I work individually with students who are poor performers to encourage higher levels of performance.
- I give students positive reinforcement for doing exemplary work. (Codde, 2007)

Once again, the outright silliness of "proving" such principles through empirical study is blatantly obvious. If students are held to higher expectations and encouraged to "excel" at their academic work, they will perform better than being in a class where the instructor could not care less about the quality of work completed. Individual instruction means more direct interaction with the student that in turn identifies potential problems such as mathematical misunderstandings, and hence learning is correspondingly enhanced. But, once again, none of these claims require empirical demonstration since they are simply matters of common sense and conceptual tautologies.

In *Curriculum Planning: A Handbook for Professionals*, Canadian scholar David Pratt (1994) provides a section on what he describes as "Twelve Principles for Effective Instruction." To quote Pratt: "The research on effective schools has yielded scores of factors that are related to instructional effectiveness. From this voluminous literature, twelve basic principles are [identified]" (p. 181). These 12 principles include such strategies as: (1) time on task; (2) motivation; (3) reading and study skills; (4) planned lessons; and (5) an orderly environment. We discuss each one of these principles through the lens Egan provides that suggests empirical research in education delivers mere analytic truths related to teaching and learning.

The idea that "time on task" enhances the quality of learning, as we pointed out earlier, seems almost too frivolous to analyse as a serious principle for effective instruction. It most surely is an analytic claim to suggest that students who spend more time learning a particular subject matter will learn more subject material. Consider the antithesis of such a claim that less time on task enhances learning; this is an absolute logical contradiction since learning, by definition, requires time spent on a particular subject matter.

Is it possible for an unmotivated student to learn? Of course, a student who lacks focus and incentive may still learn something, but it is hardly a pedagogical revelation discovered by empirical research to suggest that a motivated student will learn more material than a student of similar capability who lacks motivation. Once again, then, "research" conducted to demonstrate this idea as a principle of effective instruction seems silly, unnecessary, and an obvious waste of available human and financial resources.

The claim that reading and study skills generate enhanced learning once again suffers from the same critiques we outline earlier. An inability to read means an inability to comprehend the material in question and, hence, a corresponding inability to read will effectively reduce or eliminate learning capacity. Why empirical study would be necessary to demonstrate this point remains woefully unclear and offers another example of the waste of limited resources available to education as a whole. Finally, it is equally trivial to argue that an orderly environment creates a superior milieu for learning than a chaotic one. Thirty out-of-control students running about a classroom virtually ensures that any learning will be limited, but do we require empirical research to reach that conclusion?

In sum, Pratt's 12 principles are all reducible to what amounts to common sense about the antecedent conditions required to create a suitable and conducive environment for learning. The expenditure of millions of dollars through "voluminous" amounts of research is a testament to the waste of public funds of misguided and unnecessary investment in education research. Only by appreciating the institutional, economic, and political pressures identified by Kuhn can we even begin to understand why such a waste of public resources is permitted to continue.

5.6 Summary

Our intent in this chapter is not to attack those sincere, albeit potentially misguided, researchers in education who believe they are employing empirical methods to reach scientific conclusions, but rather to encourage them to reflect both on their methods and the practical implications of their work. Indeed, rather than creating political and institutional upheaval among faculties and department of education, our foremost intention in crafting this book is to encourage genuine and widespread self-reflection among researchers.

A tremendous financial and human resource investment is made annually by international public and private sector agencies to fund empirical research in all areas of education. Our analysis of two especially well-resourced and well-respected studies in the field of citizenship education and what are referred to as "best practices" through Egan's critical framework indicates a potentially inadequate practical return on this considerable financial and human resource investment.

In the case of civic education, it is beyond reasonable dispute that promoting tolerance, civic responsibility, community engagement, active political involvement, and critical reflection among our students, as both of the studies we explored recommend, will enrich citizenship education. However, these recommendations are simply definitions or normative descriptions of democratic citizenship. We are therefore extremely sceptical, if not entirely dismissive, about the actual contribution of empirical research in identifying and expanding these worthy democratic ideals through actual classroom practice.

The plethora of analytic conclusions drawn from this type of research in education ought to raise serious questions about the potential contribution of additional empirical studies in the field of citizenship learning and in education more generally. Ultimately, the challenge of enhancing democratic citizenship cannot be met by empirical study, but rather by teaching students the merits of the democratic values we cherish while simultaneously fostering their political voice and community engagement in our classrooms.

Our analysis of "best practices" in education reveals additional analytic connections between the findings of rather expensive research and the corresponding claims for teaching and learning. We are extremely concerned that a continued focus on empirical study will only further drain financial and intellectual resources while providing little innovative or insightful information to teachers about effective pedagogical practices. In Chapter 6, the final chapter of this book, we turn our attention to the ideological implications of scientism in education by suggesting that empirical research affords political and corporate forces with a smokescreen to distract the general public from the structural conditions that impact most directly on student academic achievement and attainment.

Chapter 6
Empirical Research as Neo-liberal Ideology

Teaching for Democratic Citizenship

6.1 Introduction

Throughout the course of this text we have made reference at several points to the distinction between science and scientism. This distinction must be appreciated to understand the ideological component of scientism and its deleterious impact on generating positive, or progressive, educational change. Science has enjoyed tremendous progress on the one hand as illustrated by the range of technological advances at our disposal within contemporary society while it simultaneously has created a range of problems that present humankind with monumental challenges. Hence, the implications of natural science are a mixed blessing, but the tangible returns generated by its methods and the technology it produces cannot be reasonably denied.

The history of human science, as we have pointed out, tells a somewhat more sordid tale, a story of profound epistemological and methodological problems. Within education, these issues are manifested in a range of claims and outcomes that are often both contradictory and confusing to academics and teachers alike (McClintock, 2007). Unlike science, the scientism pervading education is an ideology that seeks to apply the methods and practices of science to explain all elements of human experience, including teaching and learning.

In Chapter 2, we traced the early roots of scientism to the work of Auguste Comte who believed that a science of human beings was not only possible, but an absolute necessary condition of human progress. Almost two centuries later, in spite of the repeated failures confronted by social science throughout that period, many policy makers and researchers in education dogmatically adhere to the same belief that empirical methods can best resolve questions and problems pertaining to the field. Why, then, in the face of such widespread failure to generate improvement, do government officials and policy makers continue to support methods and practices that afford such little return on a huge financial and human resource investment? That is the question we attempt to answer in this final chapter.

There is of course an obvious inconsistency in many of the government initiatives and discourses supporting empirical methods in education. Those supporting science as the appropriate research paradigm in education routinely dismiss the findings of science when it comes to matters of global warming or other areas where public policy and science clash. It is painfully ironic that the same Bush administration championing the cause of empirical research in education completely ignores the plethora of data accumulated by more than 50 years of research in the sociology of education indicating the relationship between social class and educational outcomes. The sociology of education provides educators and policy developers with an abundance of empirical data about the variables that correlate most clearly with student academic achievement and attainment (Sadovnik et al., 2001). By blaming educational failure on "bad teaching" or "failing schools" any analysis of the structural inequities denying many students access to the intellectual capital consistent with academic success is avoided.

In this chapter we argue that this particular data set, perhaps the most relevant empirical data to understanding educational achievement and attainment, is ignored because it invalidates a conservative and corporate driven ideological agenda based largely on social Darwinian principles and micro-level accountability. The educational component of this socially irresponsible agenda blames student underachievement and failure on the assumed individual deficits of administrators, teachers, and students. With the focus squarely on micro-level accountability, neo-liberal ideology, and the social inequality it creates are correspondingly insulated from criticism by the absence of competing discourses and research practices. Indeed, the assumed rational capacity of science to control and shape public opinion, including the current fetish for standardized testing, has a narrowing impact on moral debate about social equality and educational opportunity within industrialized democracies. Scientism is ideologically effective, then, because it carries the influential force of science in its message without remotely challenging the primary cause of student academic failure.

In Section 6.2 we will review the various epistemological and methodological problems we have identified in educational research. In the next section, we introduce the concept of ideology by examining the work of Gramsci and other members of the so-called Frankfurt School, as well as more contemporary scholars such as Louis Althusser and Terry Eagleton. Much of our understanding of ideology as a manipulative force emerges from Marx's base/superstructure model and we will begin our discussion of ideology with a descriptive analysis of that particular component of Marxist philosophy.

In Section 6.3, we will reveal the various ways that the ideology of scientism is brought to bear on education. We explore its paralyzing impact on discourses and practices that might actually move education in more constructive directions and toward greater measures of equality, both in terms of access and academic achievement. Finally, and to conclude our efforts on a far more positive note, we will offer some suggestions we hope critical educators might adopt to begin to transform the current focus on scientism into more productive ways of actually improving education for all learners.

6.2   Summary of Research Problems in Social Science

It is worthwhile in this final chapter to summarize some of the problems we have identified in the previous pages that undermine social science and empirical research in education as legitimate fields of scientific study. A brief review of these problems will help the reader better situate the present discussion in the broader context of our previous challenge to the overall efficacy of social science methods. To appreciate the ideological component of scientism in education, we must first understand and emphasize the methodological failure of empirical research practices within education. Why do these practices endure when the problems they entail are so numerous and profound?

One general criticism of human science that we have highlighted throughout the previous chapters involves the disparate level of success and tangible returns between the natural and social sciences. This distinction ought to raise the attending question of why such a significant gap in practical return exists between the two areas if both realms actually qualify as science. Natural science has unquestionably increased our capacity to explain, predict, and manipulate (for better or worse) the world we inhabit. The comparative paralysis of social science, on the other hand, is especially salient in education where advocates of empirical research, particularly in the area of educational psychology, are hard pressed to identify any practical contribution their work has provided to improve contemporary classroom practice (Egan, 2002; Levin, 2003; McClintock, 2007).

There are of course myriad explanations offered for this failure ranging from teacher resistance to new programmes to the failure of teacher education programmes to introduce student teachers to the latest fads and slogans related to teaching and learning. However, we have argued, we hope somewhat successfully, that the lack of success experienced by empirical research and educational psychology in shaping education practice stems from a far more fundamental problem, that of a profound disconnect between the applied empirical methods of scientific inquiry and the very nature of the studied subject matter.

In many cases, we are largely convinced that the focus on educational psychology in contemporary faculties of education has actually harmed education by creating conceptual confusions around such pedagogical activities as critical and creative thinking where these terms are often reduced to confusing, unproductive, and ambiguous slogans – based on the meta-cognitive discourse – to mental "processes." Many educational psychologists, at least in their mode of language application, continue to commit the Cartesian error by mistakenly portraying activities such as critical thinking as mental processes (analysing, interpreting, evaluating, etc.) that can be taught to students in some abstract manner and then perfected through generic practice. One of us has dealt with this issue at considerable length elsewhere (Hyslop-Margison, 2005; Hyslop-Margison & Sears, 2006) so we will not rehearse the arguments here. Suffice to say that mental process terms such as critical thinking, problem solving, and creativity must be logically connected to a particular subject context. They are not "processes" or "skills" devoid of epistemic contingency and perfected through abstract practice as portrayed in much of the educational psychology literature. Like the first rule of medicine cited in the Hippocratic Oath perhaps the first axiom of good teaching should be "do no harm," an objective that might be partially achieved by avoiding precisely this type of conceptual confusion, with its negative impact on student learning, that is rampant throughout the educational psychology literature.

As we pointed out earlier in this chapter, no overarching predictive or explanatory social theories, learning theories, or theories of individual human behaviour have achieved the scientific status of general relativity or biological evolution. The contested nature of education as a discipline of inquiry guarantees that conceptual confusions will prevent absolute inferences being advanced based on observed phenomena. There is inevitably a substratum of normative commitments in education that influence how empirical judgements are interpreted. This problem in education seemingly emerges, at least in part, from a basic confusion between empirical claims on the one hand and normative claims on the other, or less charitably from the decision to simply ignore the non-empirical and messier philosophical questions of what actually constitutes quality education, intelligence, giftedness, or teaching excellence.

The investigation of education and assessing what qualifies as quality learning is a decidedly normative or philosophical enterprise, not an empirical one. Egan (2002) elucidates the difficulty of determining justified ends for the social sciences specifically as they relate to educational psychology and education more generally:

> Psychology, for all the talk of science and scientific research in education, is not a science like physics or biology. And education is unlike engineering in that education is value-saturated in ways that engineering is not. Medicine can provide the doctor with a largely unproblematic aim for intervention; such a relatively clear aim does not exist in the conceptual ferment of education, where radically different ends and purposes are vividly contested. (p.155)

As Egan suggests, the established goals in education are inevitably normative and, therefore, must be identified through moral, social, and political discussion rather than by empirical testing. These questions are what Berlin refers to as philosophical rather than empirical ones. If you recall our earlier analysis in Chapter 2, the confusion between facts and values was precisely the error Comte committed by making prescriptive judgements about the organization of human societies based on empirical study, an early and ominous warning of the confusions that were to follow. We have argued, we hope convincingly, the confusion between empirical and philosophical questions is a prevalent flaw in the social sciences that is especially common in educational research and manifested in assessments of giftedness and intelligence, and throughout standardized testing practices. This confusion has the net effect of undermining critical discussion and a more reflective analysis of the educational aims and methods most appropriate to learning within a democratic context.

Other critics of the social sciences have correctly pointed out their susceptibility to ideological bias and distortion, and to the sheer complexity of the subject matter (human beings) under investigation (Gould, 1996; Aronowitz, 1988). Some scholars suggest that searching for a systematic explanation of human and social phenomena is simply a misguided endeavour condemned to the inevitable failure it has heretofore experienced because it fails to account for human agency and free will (Miller, 1991). This point is somewhat similar in its effect if not in substance to Hume's observations more than 200 years ago that the self is a dynamic and largely unpredictable entity, a veritable bundle of sensory receptors that blunts any hope of human science delivering remotely reliable predictions. Our behaviour is spontaneous, contextual and often unpredictable.

The complexity of education as a triadic relationship makes the issue of human agency and dynamics, as well as individual differences, especially devastating problems when trying to draw generalizations from limited observed classroom phenomena. Education involves a triadic relationship that includes a teacher, students and a particular subject matter. Teachers differ dramatically in their personalities, potential pedagogical strengths, and weaknesses. Although different in what they bring to teaching and to their classrooms, these hugely different personal characteristics possessed by teachers may produce radically distinct but nevertheless successful teaching approaches. Similarly, students are dramatically different in their sensibilities, interests, learning styles, and personalities. As any well-seasoned teacher recognizes, what works with one student or group of students, or within any given particular classroom, may prove to be a near or complete disaster in another context. Finally, the subject matter itself impacts on the classroom context since one would not teach philosophy in the same manner as grammar or spelling. How are we to make any reasonable sense, then, of generic claims regarding "best practice" given the seemingly infinite variables involved?

Much of the critique we advanced in the previous pages emphasizes the fact that teaching and learning are exceptionally contextual enterprises complicated by human agency. The lack of sensitivity to this very human aspect of education, its fluidity and dynamism, inevitably leads to pedagogical inefficacy and instructional confusion and disappointment by teachers entering the profession rather than promoting their success. Indeed, it is negligent in our view to suggest to student teachers that teaching is reducible to a set of practices and skills that can be generally applied with inevitable pedagogical success. The ability of a "science" of education to capture the synergistic complexity of this triadic relationship with the dynamic human personalities and characters involved, even from an extremely sanguine point of view, is simply non-existent. In scientism, with its materialistic and deterministic assumptions, there is little remaining space for grappling with individual dynamics and spontaneous decision-making, agency, existential and creative planning or contextual sensitivity, all major imperatives and strategies of truly successful classroom teachers (Ayers, 2004).

Recently deceased and widely respected Harvard University professor Stephen Gould (1996) maintained that for all the pseudoscientific attempts to understand humans, the complexity of human behaviour is impossible to capture because of our capacity for agency and free will. Rather than accepting this inevitable feature of human experience, social scientists' methods and their related categories typically operate to define or circumscribe the subject of investigation. In other words, researchers impose preconceived conceptual frameworks and categories onto the observed phenomena rather than letting the phenomena speak for themselves. Researchers also employ descriptive language embedded with value judgements regarding their observations. We illustrated this problem with the matter of whether Jean Valjean actually "stole" a loaf of bread, or whether the behaviour in question was more correctly understood as an act of redistributive justice. Obviously, the problem of value embedded empirical descriptions and their impact on scientific objectivity is not easily dismissed.

Gould (1996) also points out the tendency of many science researchers not to report data that fails to confirm the presuppositions of their theory, another major problem in educational research. The *file-drawer effect* refers to the practice of researchers filing away or ignoring studies when outcomes fail to match their desired findings or lack consistency with past research. Although Gould is primarily concerned with this problem in natural science, the number of empirical studies in education committing this particular type of research fraud is probably significant. Indeed, we would suggest that the repression or distortion of research data is far from an uncommon feature of educational research since the focus, as Thomas Kuhn points out, is on career compatible outcomes rather than on identifying the truth.

We also illustrated, with the assistance of Louch, Smedslund, and Egan, that much of the empirical work in education affords nothing more than banal or even analytic truths. Many of the imperatives supposedly discovered by empirical research related to teaching and learning, then, offer little more than common sense techniques obvious in the complete absence of empirical study. More generally, we conclude this section by citing the views of McClintock (2007) who nicely summarizes the problem confronted by education research:

> Let's be honest and humble: because educational researchers have proven unable to exercise rigorous control and account for the relevant variables in carefully designed inquiries, their studies have had notoriously conflicting results. The direct application of research will have no coherent effects. (p. 1)

Such is the rather deplorable state of empirical research in education after more than a century and a half of ongoing application.

6.3   The Mechanisms of Ideology

A discussion of ideology must reasonably begin chronologically by briefly exploring the work of Karl Marx (1933) and, more particularly, the relationship he identified between the economic base of society and its dominant values, norms, and ideas. Indeed, most of what is termed critical theory is largely derived from Marx's nineteenth-century insights into the relationship between economics and prevailing belief systems. According to Marx, the individuals and/or values that control the economic base of a society, that includes the means of production, or the factories, the means of distribution, or the transportation networks and all of the other economic forces, will also control the prevailing ideas of the epoch or historical period. These ideas are imparted through practices such as religion, existing laws, the dominant cultural values (in the case of capitalism this would include the commodity fetish) and, most importantly for our present purposes, curricula, schools, and education.

The interaction between the base (the dominant economic interests) and the superstructure (the prevailing ideas) develops in such a way that the latter is constructed to protect the interests of the ruling class (e.g., the owners of the means of production and financial magnates). The ideas effectively reproduce the class divisions and maintain the economic privilege of the ruling class.

Schools and education, as part of the superstructure, also operate to reproduce society and, hence, protect the interests of those controlling the economic base. There are, of course, some rather obvious ways that schools fulfil this function. For example, the traditional streaming, or tracking, scheme essentially sorts students based on socio-economic class into distinct educational programmes (academic versus vocational tracks) that largely determine their future occupational or career opportunities. Students from wealthier backgrounds also typically possess certain cultural capital advantages and are, therefore, directed into college preparatory programmes. Alternatively, working class students, or students from poorer socio-economic backgrounds, tend to get streamed into programmes that limit their access to professional vocational opportunities and the higher levels of income such opportunities include. There are of course far more subtle ways, in the form of curricular content, the null curriculum and the very structure of school authority, that send powerful messages to students about their role in society as future citizens.

As Althusser (1973) appropriately points out, schools are ideally situated to wrap students in ruling ideology by exposing them to values, ideas and norms favouring the ruling class. Althusser argues that in modern capitalist society schools fulfil a major ideological role that maintains the economic power of the ruling elite even though "democracy" is generally considered the existing form of government. Democracy requires autonomous decision-making and ideology, by definition, interferes with autonomy by acting as a manipulative and indoctrinatory force shaping individual consciousness. In fact, in Althusser's (1970) view, the development of public education parallels the rise of universal democratic suffrage. With more and more members of the general population actually having a political voice in the form of electoral suffrage and the capacity to participate in state organization, Althusser suggests the aristocracy, or ruling class, was forced to develop new forms of domination over the working class. This was achieved by organizing schools and subject matter in such a way to control the consciousness, or belief systems, of future citizens and naturalize the various inequities of capitalism through public education.

Gramsci's (1971) analysis of base/superstructure interaction situates his understanding of working-class consciousness firmly within the context of ideologically oriented learning experiences in public education: "The child's consciousness is not something individual (still less individuated), and it reflects the sector of civil society in which the child participates, and the social relations which are formed within his family, his neighborhood, his village" (1971, p. 35). He elucidates further on the prescriptive and manipulative power of ideology by suggesting that, "in acquiring one's conception of the world one always belongs to a particular grouping which is that of all the social elements which share the same mode of thinking and acting. We are all conformists of some conformism or other, always man in the mass or collective man" (1971, p. 324). We are then, in his view, largely products of the ideological context in which we are immersed.

Gramsci's emphasis on the socially constructed and socially controlled nature of learning and consciousness is derived directly from his indebtedness, like so many other critical theorists, to Karl Marx. In addition to the base/superstructure, of course, one of Marx's greatest insights involved the concept of *false consciousness*, where the ideas and inclinations of working-class individuals are unauthentic and shaped by the forces of the economic base. The ideas and beliefs forming false consciousness are imposed on members of the working class by the prevailing hegemony through the various forces contained in the superstructure such as popular culture and education. As a result, learning and education, including its research practices and emphases, are always embedded within an ideological context (in the present case this is neo-liberalism). A primary function of ideology is to insulate the economic elite and protect the system supplying that privilege from any meaningful measure of criticism.

According to Gramsci (1971), education is always influenced by the relationship "of purely subjective elements with which the individual is in an active relationship" (p. 360). The structure of education, then, is directly connected to the economic and political conditions that exist at any particular time and these conditions are brought to bear on public education in any number of ways. In a capitalist society where the meager resources of the working class are exacerbated by the impact of neo-liberal economic policies, education is directed toward controlling the consciousness of not only students but the general public as well. This control is achieved in a variety of ways including, in a contemporary sense, blaming individuals rather than society for student academic failure and generally poor educational quality. Rather than viewing the social structure of opportunity as a primary unit of analysis in education, the focus of empirical research implies that the problems of educational achievement and attainment are individual, technical, and scientific rather than economic, social, or structural ones. In the process, society, and those controlling its organization escape fundamental challenges and attending public calls for the transformation of society toward greater measures of economic equality.

Terry Eagleton (1991), one of the foremost scholars in the contemporary field of the study of ideology, draws a lineage between the term and the ideals of false cognition, illusions and distortion, and mystification. He also accepts the term's employment as a way to describe more explicit forms of political discourse that simply express a particular set of beliefs. For our purposes, however, we are far more concerned with the manipulative and coercive powers of ideology that direct individuals in ways that reproduce existing hegemonic relations rather than viewing the term, in its more popular ordinary language sense, as a conscious commitment to specified values and beliefs.

One critical point Eagleton (1991) raises is that ideology "is a function of the relation of an utterance to its social context" (p. 9). An understanding of this critically important observation is crucial to grasp our central point in this chapter that empirical research in education is ideological. Empirical research, as a discourse, when applied in the context of natural science is very effective (even celebrated) both in practice and outcomes. However, when this same discourse is applied to education, its implications produce a radically different sort of consequence. Rather than generating the practical utility and technology emerging from natural science, we confront futility, confusion, and misdirection when empirical research is applied to education. Hence, using Eagleton's position as a framework for critique, the discourse of empirical research in education is demonstrably ideological because it is appropriated from one context where it functions effectively to one context where it serves prevailing hegemonic interests.

One of things that make ideologies successful is that they must resonate positively with some aspect of lived experience among the general public. Obviously, the widespread trust in science as a research mechanism and means for technical improvement is exceptionally well grounded in human experience. People relate or respond to science in a generally positive fashion and fail to understand how the discourse describing it might be used in negative or manipulative ways. Eagleton (1991) makes the point as follows: "Successful ideologies must be more than imposed illusions and for all their inconsistencies must communicate to their subjects a version of reality which is real and recognizable enough not to be simply rejected out of hand. Any ruling ideology that failed to mesh with its subjects' lived experience would be extremely vulnerable, and its exponents would be well advised to trade it in for another" (p. 15).

One of the primary features of an ideological discourse such as that surrounding empirical research in education, then, is that some of its claims are true at one level, while they are demonstrably false and manipulative at another. The claim that empirical research is scientific and effective is true in the context of the natural sciences, but deceptive and misleading in its application as it relates to research in education. Regardless, the strong general public belief in the value of science and empirical research within the natural sciences insulates its application in other areas from criticism. This insulation, of course, includes preventing the condemnation of the method as inappropriate and ineffective within the field of education.

More generally, ideology, in the critical theory tradition, can be appropriately defined as "the ideas and values that reflect and support the established order and that manifests itself in our everyday actions, decisions, and practices, usually without our being aware of its presence" (Brookfield, 2005, p. 67). But ideology is even more powerful than this since there are many instances where even though we have an underlying sense, or are even entirely conscious, of ideological manipulation we may be unable to control our impulses that direct us in ways not in keeping with our personal best interests. These impulses and the actions they precipitate serve to prop up a socio-economic system that undermines social equality. Essentially, any idea that maintains the power of the dominant group or insulates that group from critique qualifies as ideology. Clearly, scientism in education, with its instrumental focus and lack of foundational criticism, falls directly into that category.

6.4   Standardized Testing as Ideology

The standardized testing craze presently sweeping the USA and gradually making its way throughout the Canadian public education system provides an effective ideological vehicle to divert attention from the deeply rooted structural causes of student failure, and instead misdirect public contempt toward teachers, administrators, and schools. Politicians and the corporate interests they represent are protected from serious critique that challenges their wealth and power in the process. Standardized testing, with its presumption that student academic progress is quantifiable qualifies as scientism, and constitutes a discursive formation that excludes discussion or dialogue about the foundational causes of student underachievement within industrialized countries. The focus instead is directed at underachieving schools and poor quality teachers.

  If improving education is the actual goal, the approach adopted by NCLB and advocates of standardized testing is doomed to failure because it refuses to address the social causes of educational outcomes, or recognize social structure as the primary variable affecting educational outcomes. In the absence of such recognition the required structural change to improve academic achievement and attainment will never occur and, that objective, we contend ought to be the only goal of empirical academic research in education. As presently constructed, standardized testing provides a genuine distraction from addressing the kind of questions and issues that might actually equalize educational opportunity in the USA and elsewhere.

  Neo-liberal ideology portrays academic achievement as an outcome of micro-level interaction between teachers and students to distract public attention from the profound and burgeoning class inequalities of global capitalism that largely determine academic opportunity. As the corporate allies of the Bush administration dip their hands into the pockets of the poor with virtual immunity, their blood-stained tracks leaving the scene of the crime are covered up with a smokescreen discourse of educational standards, student assessment, and teacher accountability. Teachers, administrators, and schools become the convenient scapegoats for an administration that has in effect placed the US public education system under siege. The education system simply manifests the profound economic inequalities that sully American society as a whole, and as we pointed out earlier, this is the most well-established empirical correlation, but one never mentioned by the same Bush administration that supports empirical research and scientism in education, or by the advocates of NCLB.

6.5   Empirical Research and Academic Passivity

In *The Unconscious Civilization*, Canadian intellectual John Ralston Saul (1995) condemns the social sciences for contributing to the rise of political passivity among academics, another ideological influence of this type of research. In his view, the widespread compliant disposition that freezes anti-hegemonic action found among social science researchers is because they "still labour under the burden of false sciences" (p. 69). Saul articulates the problem this way:

> Their experiments do not provide any measurable progress in the manner of a real science. In place of real evidence they are obliged to pile up overwhelming weights of documenta- tion relating to human action – none of which is proof, little of it even illustration. This sort of material carries the force of neither history nor creativity. What they are working with is circumstantial evidence. They claim to produce truths, but these truths are too fragile to produce anything other than passivity. (p. 69)

The end product of this passivity, emerging from the contradictory claims and findings of social science research, is that universities, once centres of active public and social criticism, a crucial role within a truly democratic society, are often reduced to institutional vehicles advancing the neo-liberal causes of economic globalization and technological jingoism under the banner of science and technical rationality.

The social sciences generally and education in particular provide the bulwark for an entire ideological movement consistent with scientism. Many academics often pressured and reeling under the institutional expectations of grant writing, scholarship, service, and teaching, find themselves in increasingly compliant and passive positions when dealing with university administrators and government officials. They have become, as Stanley Aronowitz (2001) so poignantly describes them, little more than clerical proletariat labour. The pressure to procure research grants, as we pointed out through the work of Thomas Kuhn in an earlier chapter, encourages researchers to operate within the confines of existing theoretical constructs to achieve recognition of their work among their peers rather than seriously address the root causes of education failure.

There are many academics within our own educational research community who derive significant practical and professional benefit from the present focus on scientific research in education. Research projects, ongoing support of scientific meetings and seminars, and the funding of institutions and careers create an interrelated set of subcultures dependent on empirical methods of inquiry. Most academics are obviously reluctant to bite the hand that feeds them, or take overt actions that may undermine their tenure and professional success.

The ensuing political and academic disconnect of genuinely human studies and moral discourse from academia, combined with the gross and intentional under- funding of research relative to such inquiry, prioritizes blind technological develop- ment and empirical research at the expense of meaningful debate about creating a better, more just and caring world that includes fundamental structural changes to public education systems. This, we fear, is the unfortunate legacy of scientism in education within a neo-liberal order.

6.6   Scientism as Ideology

From the beginning of this book we have indicated our desire to make one point abundantly clear. We employ the word scientism rather than science because this book is not an attack on science, its methods or practices, but our objective is to raise some extremely important questions about the ideology of scientism. Again, scientism is the belief that scientific approaches to all problems or issues will inevitably deliver the best possible available outcomes. Scientism is also ideological in the critical theory application of the term since it protects the prevailing hegemony from transformative analysis.

We retain considerable epistemic faith, supported by a significant measure of accumulated evidence, in a mediated version of scientific realism. Science may not present us with an Archimedean view of the natural world around us, but considering our shared conceptual framework – our Kantian conceptual goggles and shared range of conceptual description – it represents a distinctly human understanding of that world offering both practical utility and a reasonable basis for what we describe as "facts" and "truth." From an epistemological and pragmatic perspective, the tools and practices of natural science work exceptionally well in fields such as physics, chemistry, and medicine. They allow us to make reliable predictions concerning the behaviours of bodies in motion, the interaction of various carbon compounds and chemical elements, and the probable health effects of recently developed pharmaceuticals. Although beset with many errors throughout the ages, natural science has, more or less, progressively offered increasingly accurate and comprehensive knowledge about the world around us. This claim, it seems to us, is relatively unproblematic.

Scientism, on the other hand, is based on a blind ideological commitment or dogmatic thinking rather than on demonstrable epistemological progress. It abounds in educational research and scholarship under the guise of science not because of its proven track record of success since, quite to the contrary and as we have demonstrated throughout these pages, there is no such track record available, but because its adoption and application leads to funded proposals for research grants, promotes research agendas, and secures referred publications within research journals. To put it mildly, scientism in education represents a growth industry with abundant returns for those academics and researchers willing to pursue its practices while remaining dangerously blind to its multitude of follies.

Within the present milieu of scientism, educational research outside its narrow purview is often dismissed as without basis or value and, in many cases, therefore not worthy of funding or publication. Those academics pursuing scholarly work or publishing outside the empirical realm may experience great difficulty in convincing their colleagues that their scholarship has any significant measure of value or applicability. Further, their opportunity to secure external funding for their work is significantly reduced. It is of no small importance that as we write this final chapter, the Social Sciences and Humanities Research Council of Canada (SSHRC) is introducing even tougher guidelines to ensure funded proposals employ "scientific" practices. By exploring the work of Thomas Kuhn, we elaborated on this problem and the coercive forces it generates to compel academics to comply with the prevailing research paradigm. In the process, the academic energy focused on addressing foundational questions regarding education is correspondingly reduced.

Scientism represents a view of the world that places its trust in scientific progress and only in scientific progress regardless of the context or subject matter. Scientism, perhaps flourishing more than ever in the enduring spirit of Comte's original positivist mission, is a powerful ideological force and now represents, according to many policy makers and researchers, the only available practice leading to possible social or educational progress (National Research Council, 2002). Scientism represents a belief that scientific knowledge is the foundation of all knowledge and that, consequently, scientific argument should always be weighed far more heavily than other forms of argument such as moral argument. Scientism is especially successful in muting debates, including moral discussion about schools and society, that fail to fit a scientific framework, or whose argument fails to meet the empirical standards of scientific inquiry. Scientism rejects other methods because it holds that all fields of inquiry, including the study of human beings and education, should be subject to, and are best understood by, the standard scientific methods of investigation. In this book, we hope to have demonstrated that this view, when applied to education in particular, produces some very unfortunate, negative, and even quite dangerous consequences.

In spite of the current and misguided faith in scientism, especially in education, contemporary natural science confronts an astonishing ideological paradox. Whereas science is the misguided practice selected for improving education, its findings in other areas where its methods are legitimately applied are routinely dismissed by a Bush administration controlled largely by its neo-conservative and evangelical Christian political base. For example, the same Bush administration that advocates rigorous scientific methods be applied to education constantly interferes with the findings of natural science in such areas as evolution, global warming, and genetic engineering, even when the latter obviously holds tremendous promise for curing numerous human diseases.

Why, then, is the same US administration that routinely rejects the findings of natural science so stricken with the idea of science as a means to improve educational outcomes? Natural science tends to undermine the metaphysical assumptions supporting the religious fundamentalism driving significant portions of the Bush presidential agenda and its political base. However, the application of science in the educational arena is acceptable because educational psychology focuses on the failure or shortcomings of schools, teachers, and administrators rather than on the profound social injustices of neo-liberal stratification that impact deleteriously and more generally on student academic achievement and attainment. In other words, it places the focus of educational failure on individuals rather than on the social structure of opportunity, a powerful ideological tool.

In our neo-liberal context, then, we are compelled to conclude that it is not so much that science as a general practice is being supported but rather a deception is being advanced based on *scientism* that promotes certain conservative and corporate ideological commitments. As Schwandt points out: "The Bush administration insert[s] itself into various ventures in order to spin, suppress, and manipulate findings of scientific investigation on a variety of topics – all in the name of scientific integrity" (cited in Howe, 2005, p. 241). In spite of the plethora of credible evidence from many of world's leading scientists, including Canada's David Suzuki (2005), warnings about the catastrophic dangers following from the problem of global warming are routinely ignored. By turning a deaf ear to such warnings, the Bush administration refuses to accept the demonstrably scientific conclusion that the planet is warming up at an alarming rate and to an already dangerous degree. When science does not mesh with the corporate, religious and neo-conservative assumptions and interests driving US politics, then it is simply written off as "faulty science" or perhaps simply science better off ignored. Clearly, science is the method of choice for the Bush administration and its followers only when its application supports the ideological agenda of the neo-liberal and neo-conservative economic hegemony.

Part of our mission in writing this book, then, is simply advising the emperor, in this case a rather suitable metaphor for the blind faith existing among educational researchers that science affords the best vehicle to achieve educational improvement, that so-called scientific researchers in education are actually "wearing no clothes." Indeed, this metaphor seems especially appropriate for this situation since the vested interest inextricably bound up within scientific and empirical study is of considerable magnitude, a situation that makes ignoring the truth about social science research far easier than confronting it. Whereas a lack of tangible success might normally prompt the search for better ideas and theories about improving education, the politics, economics and ideology of scientism are deeply embedded in education research, and supported by an extremely well-developed and highly dependent academic infrastructure. Entire "empires." and we are being quite literate in our use of this term, of researchers, institutions, research expertise and related funding opportunities rely on the appropriateness of science as a vehicle to enhance classroom practice. In the final analysis, we obviously believe it is an approach that continues to do far more damage to education than good.

The naturalization of neo-liberal ideology is also widely evident in a range of contemporary curricula that typically describe present circumstances to students in terms that suggest either their inevitability or social desirability. Neo-liberal ideology removes the economic sphere from moral or social discussion by portraying these latter realms of discourse as entirely dependent on the former. In other words, appropriate social, moral and educational action and policy is determined by what works for the market, and what works for the market, according to the prevailing logic, is neo-liberalism. All other spheres of life are correspondingly designed to address the needs of the marketplace and any interference with market logic becomes inconceivable let alone possible. Habermas (1996) argues that we are witnessing the total invasion of what he describes as the *life world* by the ideological creation of false needs and the decline of pubic spaces. The life world for Habermas consists of those fundamental human experiences and interactions that generate a sense of peace or individual well-being, and provide the necessary community and intellectual space for critical democratic discussion. The provision of such space has been one of the traditional objectives of public education, especially higher education that scientism potentially threatens by reducing all meaningful questions to empirically answerable ones.

With the revised role of government in neo-liberalism reduced to that of creating optimum market conditions, public policy development faced concerted attack in the final two decades of the twentieth century. Nationally owned resources and services were routinely sold to the private sector predicated on the view that such sell offs would necessarily increase productive efficiency. Public education did not escape the shift toward privatization as evidenced by the growth of the school choice movement, especially in the USA. Consistent with the unquestioned faith in competition and micro-level accountability as the means to correct all possible social and economic ills, neo-liberalism demanded that schools and teachers be held directly accountable for student academic fortunes through the development of standardized testing. As an ideological mechanism, these tests effectively mask the structural causes of academic underachievement and unemployment by viewing educational problems as individual rather than social failures. With complete disregard for resource inequity, economic disparity, and other structural impediments to education, the belief developed, encouraged by private enterprise that education could be improved by creating a parallel charter schooling system to compete with the public variety. Once again, this trend simply represents another distraction from the fundamental structural problems influencing student learning outcomes.

In spite of their traditional role as the gatekeepers of intellectual freedom, universities have not escaped the drift toward human capital preparation and other instrumental demands of the marketplace. Faced with huge public expenditure reductions, universities are increasingly becoming institutions focused on technical training rather than on creating informed and engaged democratic citizens (Giroux, 2004). At one of our own institutions, Concordia University, programmes are marketed under the slogan "real education for the real world." an idea that effectively reduces learning to social efficiency precepts by implying there actually is a real social world beyond that shaped by human agency and decision-making. In the USA, a significant number of research chairs are entirely corporate sponsored with the attending obligation to direct research agendas toward issues that pay corporate dividends (Aronowitz, 2001).

Increasingly, universities describe their relationship with students within a business model framework as that of clients or customers of the university rather than as members of a scholarly or intellectual community with rights and responsibilities related to shaping public life. A recent article appearing in a University of Toronto publication extolled that university's new focus on students as customers who deserved good service as a smart move not for delivering quality education but for nurturing long-term alumni loyalty – and presumably financial contributions (Hyslop-Margison & Sears, in press). This commodification of education shows up not only in marketing and customer service campaigns directed at students, parents, and alumni, but in an increasing focus on universities as providers of commodities (under the guise of credentials) rather than education. Almost 40 years ago social critic Ivan Illich argued that Western educational institutions had already substituted credentialing for educating, an observation that seems even truer today (Hyslop-Margison & Sears, in press).

Current reductions in public funding for universities precipitate intense competition between faculty for available private and public grants. The ability to attract funding into the university is now typically viewed as a fundamental tenure requirement. The research funded by these grants often poses little challenge to the neo-liberal structure because it either neglects society as a primary unit of analysis or manifestly embraces prevailing human capital objectives. The focus of this research is often grounded far more in the idea of social and economic utility than in fostering democratic critique. The idea that a university experience is about intellectual growth, social debate, and democratic dialogue has been largely usurped by the neo-liberal objectives of customer service, credentializing, technical training, and instrumental learning. In the current university milieu, faculty are often reduced from their democratic role of social critic or public intellectual to that of entrepreneurial researcher.

The ability and right to criticize public figures and government policy is obviously central to university life and democratic societies. In the post September 11, 2001, USA it has become dangerously unpopular for educators at all levels to criticize the Bush administration's current direction and decision-making on domestic and foreign policy. Those public figures and academics who do so, such as recently illustrated by the case featuring University of Colorado professor Ward Churchill, run the risk of either personal attack or, in this particular case, the almost complete ruination of one's professional reputation. Giroux (2004) refers to the present political context as *emergency time*, or a period during which the general public is easily manipulated through fear and anxiety to accept government action and policy that it would otherwise reject. Emergency time creates a period when criticism of government policy, even in US academic circles, is rejected as being counter to a conception of a greater public "good." and civil liberties are undermined without public criticism as state and corporate power correspondingly increase.

It is critically important that universities respect and protect the democratic right of individual dissent so long as that dissent does not explicitly threaten the well-being of other citizens. The public space for social critique must be protected even when such dissent runs counter to mainstream or popular thinking. Obviously, no one is obligated to accept Ward Churchill's controversial contention that the financial bureaucrats situated in the World Trade Center who succumbed to the unfortunate terrorist attacks were akin to "little Eichmans" but he deserves the opportunity to state that belief and support it on the basis of some attending argument. To reject the position, as so many have both outside and inside the academic arena, simply on the grounds that it is "offensive" or counter to generally held public opinion undermines the basic principles of democratic and intellectual discourse. The attack on Professor Churchill symbolically reflects a growing and profoundly disturbing trend within the USA that routinely persecutes or ridicules anyone who challenges neo-liberal ideology or questions US foreign policy. Within such a milieu, thick, or authentic, democracy is endangered because the scope of circulating ideas and public debate is narrowed to predetermined assumptions and objectives that comply with a narrow point of view. Even those holding counter perspectives tend to withhold their views under such conditions due to fear of subsequent persecution. Thankfully, with the recent shift in US political power, new spaces are seemingly appearing that allow for more trenchant critiques of the Bush administration's domestic and foreign policy decisions, although voiced mainstream alternatives advanced by Democratic Party leadership hopefuls still remain disturbingly ambiguous.

6.7 Education for Democratic Citizenship

An education system designed to respond to the needs of the marketplace predictably appears radically different from one focused on preparing students for the responsibilities of democratic citizenship. The No Child Left Behind (NCLB) legislation in the USA, for example, does not contain a single reference to either democracy or democratic citizenship. Neo-liberal culture is naturalized to students in public and higher education as an unchangeable social reality rather than critiqued as an ideological movement imposed by special corporate interests on citizens of industrialized democratic societies. Outside the strictures of the global market, education in the neo-liberal order conveys to students there are simply no longer any meaningful choices to be made. Throughout contemporary career education curricula in particular, and in a variety of ideologically manipulative ways, students are expected to prepare for an uncertain occupational future and are discursively convinced that such conditions are beyond the scope of their own political agency. Pedagogical tools of social critique such as critical thinking, lifelong learning, and critical literacy are all influenced by the neo-liberal shift toward instrumental instruction. As a result, schools fail to prepare students as democratic citizens who possess the necessary understanding and dispositions to decide politically between various social possibilities. Instead, students are portrayed as mere objects in history and ideologically inculcated with a consumer-driven worldview devoid of imagination, hope, or alternative social visions.

Consistent with the neo-liberal assumptions propelling reform in education, many organizations influencing contemporary policy development within education advance a human capital construct of lifelong learning designed to address unstable labour market conditions (Hyslop-Margison & Naseem, in press). Contemporary labour market conditions generally include recurrent occupational displacement and instability that combine to undermine the job security of workers. The human capital construct of lifelong learning is designed to ensure that students, as future workers, passively accept the occupational uncertainty they will inevitably confront in the new global economic order. For example, the World Bank Group endorses the following concept of lifelong learning:

In the 21st century, workers need to be lifelong learners, adapting continuously to changed opportunities and to the labour market demands of the knowledge economy. Lifelong learning is more than education and training beyond formal schooling. A comprehensive programme of lifelong-learning education for dynamic economies, within the context of the overall development framework of each country, encompasses all levels. (The World Bank, 2004)

From this perspective, lifelong learning involves the constant upgrading of skills to ensure workers remain responsive to contemporary labour market demands. By blurring the distinction between the constructed nature of society and natural reality, thus ignoring Searle's crucial distinction between brute facts and social facts, this discourse conveys to students that their role is simply preparing for an inevitable and unstable future rather than engaging with or democratically transforming their political, economic, and social landscapes (Searle, 1995).

We believe the stakes in the battle for lifelong learning are enormously high. The human capital discourse portraying lifelong learning as a labour market adjustment strategy undermines the ability of students to act as democratic agents of social change. Democratic forms of pedagogy view humans and society as unfinished, subject to continual evaluation and transformation. As dynamic subjects in history, students, respected as lifelong learners, have a right to influence economic conditions and, in the process, create a more just, stable and caring social experience. From a democratic perspective, then, we should not ask our students to accept an ahistorical view of the world that represents social reality and labour market conditions as fixed and unchangeable, and reduces their role to mere social adaptation (Hyslop-Margison & Naseem, in press). Rather they should be encouraged to critique and challenge contemporary values with social transformation conveyed as a genuine democratic possibility.

The area of literacy education represents another example where the instrumental assumptions of neo-liberal ideology dominate the curriculum. The 1998 Ontario Secondary Schools Detailed Discussion Document issued by the Ministry of Education explored several possible purposes for education that eventually precipitated large-scale curricular reform in the Canadian province. These purposes range from preparing students for the workforce to preparing students as reflective individuals and engaged democratic citizens. The Ontario Ministry of Education (1998) concluded that meeting both of these objectives required enhancing the literacy "skills" of students. In a ministry brochure titled "Literacy in Ontario: The Rewards are for Life." the functionalist assumptions supporting the ministry's vision of literacy are revealed: "Literacy skills are needed every day – at work, at home, at school, in the community. These skills help people to take part in further education and training, as well as to find and keep jobs." The emphasis on simply encoding textual messages for instrumental workplace application without considering the broader social context from which that information emerges undermines the democratic participation of learners by ignoring their role as rational agents in social construction (Hyslop-Margison & Pinto, in press).

The political perspective represented in many of the current literacy practices in the province of Ontario and elsewhere reveals a monolithic neo-liberal agenda that denies students access to alternative worldviews. This agenda interferes with the fundamental democratic right of students to act as political agents of social reconstruction by transforming the social, economic, and labour market circumstances they confront. Students are depicted by literacy imperatives as objects of, rather than subjects in, the construction of social reality. Freire (1970) explains how critical forms of literacy learning counteract this type of politically paralyzing and decidedly undemocratic education: "In problem-posing education, [students] develop their power to perceive critically the way they exist in the world with which and in which they find themselves; they come to see the world not as static reality, but as a reality in process, in transformation" (p. 78). In critical literacy, students learn to give democratic voice to the vocational and social challenges they presently confront and develop a deep understanding that social change is a real possibility. This understanding is central to the democratic learning advocated by Freire who "taught us that, for social transformation to take place, it is important for students to understand and give voice to their personal struggles" (Darder, 2002, p. 155).

Throughout Ontario education imperatives, students presently learn to view and name the world through a corporate dominated discourse that conveys particular values, assumptions, and expectations. Alternatively, the primary objective of critical literacy in democratic education that resists the indoctrinatory forces of neoliberalism is heightening student awareness on how discourse influences our values and our view of social reality. Apple (2000) describes this alternate conception as "critical literacy, powerful literacy, political literacy which enables the growth of genuine understandings and control of all the spheres of social life in which we participate" (p. 42).

Even in the area of critical thinking, current curriculum constructs tend toward an instrumental reasoning approach that ignores the social and economic context as a primary unit of analysis. Critical thinking is widely portrayed as a generic problem-solving strategy to generate technical solutions within a naturalized market economy system. Five Steps to Better Critical Thinking, Problem Solving, and Decision-Making, for example, a business resource created for teachers, emphasizes the daily practical challenges that workers might expect to confront: "Some problems are big and unmistakable, such as the failure of an airfreight delivery service to get packages to customers on time. Other problems may be continuing annoyances, such as regularly running out of toner for an office copy machine" (Guffey, 1996).

British Columbia's Business Education reflects a technical rationality focus more directly by suggesting that: "Critical thinking is an important aspect of all courses. Instruction should include opportunities for students to justify positions on issues and to apply economic and business principles to particular circumstances" (British Columbia Ministry of Education, 1998). The Iowa City Community School District Career/Business Education high school curriculum describes problem solving as "an employability skill required by employers" (Iowa City Community School District, 2003) The Missouri Department of Elementary and Secondary Education's Division of Vocational and Adult Education maintain that critical thinking skills help students "solve everyday, practical problems" (Missouri Department of Elementary and Secondary Education, 2003).

These critical thinking constructs promote technical rationality and instrumental reasoning by encouraging students to address problems from a limited perspective that ignores wider workplace, labour market, and socio-economic issues. When students are tacitly or openly discouraged from engaging the social and economic forces shaping contemporary experience, their democratic right to participate in directing these forces is correspondingly undermined. Indeed, the moral imperatives of education within a democratic society require that students are provided with the necessary knowledge and dispositions to make informed choices about current political and social conditions, and entertain possible alternatives to improve these conditions (Hyslop-Margison & Armstrong, 2004).

One of the most interesting curricular vehicles for truncating students' ability to participate as agents in shaping their world is the return of civics to the school curriculum. Both Ontario and British Columbia recently reintroduced civics courses to the high school curriculum under neo-liberal governments; Mike Harris's government in Ontario and Gordon Campbell's in British Columbia (Ontario Ministry of Education, 2005; British Columbia Ministry of Education, 2005). While both of these curricula take a generally activist approach to citizenship and focus on encouraging citizen engagement, an idea we applaud, the move to centralize citizenship education in civics courses rather than infusing it more widely in the curriculum implies that civic action ought to be limited to the overtly political sphere and does not include action to shape economic systems, society more generally, or vocational experience (Hyslop-Margison & Sears, in press). Scientism will not lead us to the educational outcomes, described above but political will combined with curricular change very well could produce learning outcomes consistent with authentic democratic citizenship.

6.8   Conclusion

Our modest intent in this book has not been to attack those sincere, albeit misguided, researchers in education who believe they are employing empirical methods to reach scientific conclusions, but rather to encourage them to reflect on their methods, and the practical and moral implications of their venture. The only genuine solutions to problems of low student achievement and attainment require addressing the moral imperatives of social justice and equality of opportunity within our societies. Educational researchers must move beyond mere empirical practices that deflect attention from such matters, and become part of the political struggle for the fairer distribution of economic resources within our society.

The proponents of empirical methods, gleefully advancing their positivist ideological agenda, presently dictate what counts as sensible, believable, and meaningful in educational research. Indeed, the ideologues advancing this position routinely exclude and ridicule educational research that offers radical dissent to the hegemony of scientism. Their considerable success in curtailing intellectual debate by invalidating non-scientific dialogue poses a genuine threat to the moral underpinnings of our democratic society. By exposing a few of the technical weaknesses of pseudoscientific research in education, we hope to stimulate discussion and debate that moves researchers toward more human studies, and more moral and democratic methods of educational inquiry. In short we hope to stem the current tide of scientism sweeping over education and restore our discipline to a legitimate area of study with the power to transform the structural problems impeding the academic achievement of so many young and vulnerable students. The call for change is a clarion one that requires our immediate and forthright response.

References

Althusser, L. (1970). *For marx*. New York: Vintage Books.

Althusser, L. (1973). Ideology and the state. In: L. Althusser (Ed.). *Essays on ideology* (pp. 1–61). London: The Thetford Press.

Amadeo, J., Torney-Purta, J., Lehman, R., Hursfeldt, V., & Niklova, R. (2002). *Civic knowledge and engagement: An IEA study of upper secondary students in sixteen countries*. Amsterdam: International Association for the Evaluation of Educational Achievement.

American Educational Research Association. (2001). *Handbook of research on teaching*. 4th edn. V. Richardson (Ed.). Washington, DC: Author.

Apple, M. (2000). *Official knowledge: Democratic education in a conservative age*. 2nd edn. New York: Routledge.

Aquinas, T. (1951). *Summa theologica*. Chicago, IL: Regnery.

Aronowitz, S. (1988). *Science as power: Discourse and ideology in modern society*. Minneapolis, MN: University of Minnesota Press.

Aronowitz, S. (2001). *The last good job in America*. New York: Rowman & Littlefield.

Ayer, A. J. (1952). *Language, truth and logic*. New York: Dover.

Ayer, A. J. (1975) *Central question of philosophy*, London: Weidenfield & Nicholson.

Ayer, A. J. (1959). *Logical positivism*. London: Allen & Unwin.

Ayers, W. (2004). *Teaching toward freedom: Moral commitment and ethical action in the classroom*. Boston, MA: Beacon Press.

Bacon, F. (1963). *Novum organum*. Oxford: Clarendon Press.

Ball, S. J. (1997). Policy sociology and critical social research: A personal review of recent education policy and policy research. *British Educational Research Journal, 23*(1), 251–271.

Barnes, B. (1982). *T. S. Kuhn and social science*. New York: Columbia University Press.

Barrow, R. (1981). *The philosophy of schooling*. New York: Wiley.

Barrow, R. (1984). *Giving teaching back to teachers: A critical introduction to curriculum theory*. London, ONT: Althouse Press.

Barrow, R. (1995). For whom the bell tolls. *Alberta Journal of Educational Research, 41*(3), 289–296.

Berlin, I. (1962). Does political theory still exist? In: P. Laslett & W. Runciman (Eds.). *Philosophy, politics, society*. Oxford: Basil Blackwell.

Bernstein, R. J. (1978). *The reconstruction of social and political thought*. New York: Harcourt Brace & Jvovanovich.

Bernstein, R. J. (1991) *The new constellation: The ethical-political horizons of modernity/post-moderntiy*. Cambridge: Polity Press.

Biesta, G. J. & Burbules, N. C. (2003). *Pragmatism and educational research*. Landam. MD: Rowman & Littlefield.

British Columbia Ministry of Education. (1998). *Business education*. Victoria, BC: Author.

British Columbia Ministry of Education. (2005). *Civic studies 11*. Victoria, BC: Author.

Brookfield, S. (2005). *The power of critical theory: Liberating adult learning and teaching.* San Francisco, CA: Jossey-Bass.

Cazeneuve, J. (1972). *Luciene Levy-Bruhl.* Oxford: Basil Blackwell.

Chickering, A. & Gamson, Z. (1991). *Applying the seven principles for good practice in undergraduate education.* San Francisco, CA: Jossey-Bass.

Codde, J. (2007). Applying the seven principles for good practice in undergraduate education. Retrieved April 01, 2007, from www.msu.edu/user/coddejos/seven.htm

Comte, A. (1974). *The positivist philosophy.* New York: AMS Press.

Conference Board of Canada. (2001). *Employability skills profile.* Ottawa, Canada: Author.

Corvi, R. (1996). *An introduction to the thought of Karl Popper.* New York: Routledge.

Counihan, T. (1986). Epistemology and science: Feyerabend and Lecourte. *Economy and Society, 5,* 1.

Craig, R., Kerr, D., Wade, P., & Taylor, G. (2004). *Taking post-16 citizenship forward: Learning from the post -16 citizenship development projects.* Norwich, UK: Queen's Printer.

Darder, A. (2002). *Reinventing paulo freire: A pedagogy of love.* Boulder, CO: Westview Press.

Denzin, N. (1997) *Interpretive ethnography: Ethnographic practices for the 21st century.* Thousand Oaks, London, New Delhi: Sage.

Denzin, N. & Lincoln, Y. (1998) *Strategies of qualitative inquiry.* Thousand Oaks, London, New Delhi: Sage.

Dewey, J. (1916). *Democracy and education.* New York: The Free Press.

Donovan, S., Bransford, J. D., & Pellgrino, J. (1999). *How people learn: Bridging research and practice.* Washington, DC: National Academic Press.

Durkheim, E. (1963). *Selections from his work. Introduction and commentaries by G. Simpson.* New York: Crowell.

Durkheim, E. (1982). *The rules of the sociological method.* New York: Free Press.

Durkheim, E. (1994). *Durkheim on religion.* Atlanta, GA: Scholars Press.

Eagleton, T. (1991). *Ideology: An introduction.* London: Verso.

Egan, K. (2002). *Getting it wrong from the beginning: Our progressivist heritage from Herbert Spencer, John Dewey and Jean Piaget.* New Haven, CT: Yale University Press.

Erickson, F. (2005). Arts, humanities, and sciences in education research and social engineering in federal education policy. *Teachers College Record, 107*(1), 4–9.

Fenstermacher, G. D. (1979). A philosophical consideration of recent research on teacher effectiveness. *Review of Research in Education, 6,* 157–185.

Feyerabend, P. (1975) *Against method.* London: New Left Books.

Frege, G. (1892). On sense and reference. In: P. Geach & M. Black (Eds.). *Translations from the philosophical writings of Gottlob Frege.* Oxford: Blackwell.

Freire, P. (1970). *Pedagogy of the oppressed.* New York: Herder & Herder.

Friedman, M. (1999). *Reconsidering logical positivism.* Cambridge: Cambridge University Press.

Foucault, M. (1991). What is enlightenment? In: P. Rabinow (Ed.). *The Foucault reader* (pp. 32–50). Harmondsworth, UK: Penguin.

Gall, M. D., Borg, W. R., & Gall, J. (1996). *Educational research: An introduction.* New York: Longman.

Giroux, H. (2004). *The abandoned generation: Democracy beyond the culture of fear.* New York: Palgrave.

Gorton, W. A. (2006). *Karl Popper and the social sciences.* Albany, NY: State University of New York Press.

Gould, S. (1996). *The mismeasure of man.* New York: W. W. Norton.

Gramsci, A. (1971). *Selections from the prison notebooks.* London: Lawrence & Wishart.

Gross, R. (1987). *Psychology: The science of mind and behaviour.* London: Hodder & Stoughton.

Guffey, M. (1996). *Business communication: Process and product.* Cincinnati, OH: South-Western College Publishing.

Habermas, J. (1970). *Toward a rational society*. Boston, MA: Beacon Press.

Habermas, J. (1996). *Debating the state of philosophy*. Westport, CT: Praeger.

Hammersley, M. (1992). *What's wrong with ethnography?* London: Routledge.

Hempel, C. G. (1965). *Aspects of scientific explanation, and other essays in the philosophy of science*.

Hempel, C. G. (1966). *Philosophy of natural science*. Englewood, CA: Prentice-Hall.

Herrstein, R. J. & Murray, C. (1994). *The bell curve: Intelligence and class structure in American life*. New York: Free Press.

Hirsch, E. D. (2001). Romancing the child. *Education Matters*, Spring, 34–39.Howe, K. (2005). The education science question: A symposium. *Educational Theory*, 55(3), 235–244.

Hume, D. (2000). *Enquiries concerning human understanding and concerning the principles of morals*. Oxford: Clarendon Press.

Hyslop-Margison, E. J. & Armstrong, J. (2004). Critical thinking in career education: The democratic importance of foundational rationality. *Journal of Career and Technical Education*, 21(1), 39–49.

Hyslop-Margison, E. J. (2005). Liberalizing vocational study: Democratic approaches to career education. Landham, MD: University Press of America.

Hyslop-Margison, E. J. & Naseem, A. (in press). Career education as humanization: A Freirean approach to lifelong learning. *Alberta Journal of Educational Research*.

Hyslop-Margison, E. J. & Pinto, L. (in press). Critical literacy for democratic learning in career education. *Canadian Journal of Education*.

Hyslop-Margison, E. J. & Richardson, T. (2005). Rethinking progressivism and the crisis of liberal humanism: Historical and contemporary perspectives on education for democratic citizenship. *International Journal of Progressive Education*, 1(2), 31–48.

Hyslop-Margison, E. J. & Sears, A. (2006). *Neo-liberalism, globalization and human capital learning: Reclaiming education for democratic citizenship*. Dordrecht, The Netherlands: Springer.

Hyslop-Margison, E. J. & Sears, A. (in press). International citizenship education. In: M. Peters, H. Blee, P. Enslin, & A. Britton (Eds.). *Handbook of global citizenship education*. Rotterdam, The Netherlands: Sense.

International Association for the Evaluation of Educational Achievement (IEA). (2005). *Civic Education Study*. Retrieved July 15, 2005, from //www2.h-berlin.de/empir_bf/iea_e1.html

Iowa City Community School District. (2003). Career/Business Education. Retrieved July 10, 2003, from www.iowa.city.k12.ia.us/newinfo/careered.html

Kaestle, C. (1993). The awful reputation of educational research. *Educational Researcher*, 22(1), 23–31.

Kant, I. (1934). *The critique of pure reason*. London: J. M. Dent & Sons.

Keuth, H. (2005). *The philosophy of Karl Popper*. New York: Cambridge University Press.

Kuhn, T. (1970) *The structure of scientific revolutions*. Chicago, IL: University of Chicago Press.

Kuhn, T. (1977). Objectivity, value judgment and theory choice. In: *The essential tension* (pp. 320–339). Chicago, IL: University of Chicago Press.

Kuhn, T. (1998). The natural and the human sciences. In: E. D. Klemke, R. Hollinger, D. Rudge, & D. Kline (Eds.). *Introductory readings in the philosophy of science*. 3rd edn. New York: Prometheus Books.

Labov, W. (1970). The logic of non-standard English. In: F. Williams (Ed.). *Language and poverty: Perspectives on a theme*. Chicago, IL: Markham.

Lagemann, E. C. (1999). An auspicious moment for educational research. In: E. C. Lagemann & L. S. Shulman (Eds.). *Issues in educational research: Problems and possibilities*. San Francisco, CA: Jossey-Bass.

Laird, J. (1967). *Hume's philosophy of human nature*. Hamden, CT: Archon Books.

Lather, P. (1991). *Getting smart*. New York: Routledge.

Lather, P. (2004). This is your father's paradigm: Government intrusion and the case of qualitative research in education. *Qualitative Inquiry*, 10(1), 15–34.

Lave, J. & Wenger, E. (1991). *Situated learning: Legitimate peripheral participation*. Cambridge: Cambridge University Press.

Levin, B. (2003, November). Improving research-policy relationships: Lessons from the case of literacy. Paper presented at the OISE/UT International Conference on Literacy Policies for the Schools We Need, Toronto, Canada.

Levy-Bruhl, L. (1925). *How natives think*. New York: A. A. Knopf.

Louch, A. R. (1966). *Explanation and human action*. Berkeley, CA: University of California Press.

Lyotard, J. F. (1997). *Postmodern fables*. Minneapolis, MN: University of Minnesota Press.

Marcuse, H. (1964). *One dimensional man: Studies in the ideology of advanced industrial society*. Boston, MA: Beacon Press.

Marx, K. (1933). *Capital: A critique of political economy*. London: J. M. Dent.

Marzano, R. J., Pickering, D. J., & Pollock, J. E. (2001). *Classroom instruction that works*. Alexandria, VA: Association for Supervision and Curriculum Development.

Maykut, P. & Moorehouse, R., (1994). *Beginning qualitative research: A philosophical and practical guide*. London, Washington, DC: The Falmer Press.

Maxwell, J. A. (2004). Causal explanation, qualitative research, and scientific inquiry in education. *Educational Researcher, 33*(2), 3–11.

McClintock, R. (2007). Educational research. *Teachers College Record*. Retrieved April, 5, 2007, from http://www.tcrecord.org

McLaren, P. (2003). *Life in schools: An introduction to critical pedagogy in the foundations of education*. 4th edn. Boston, MA: Allyn & Bacon.

Miller, R. W. (1991). Fact and method in the social sciences. In: R. Boyd, P. Gasper, & J. D. Trout (Eds.). *Philosophy of science*. Cambridge, MA: MIT Press.

Missouri Department of Elementary and Secondary Education. (2003). *Family and consumer sciences curriculum*. Retrieved October 22, 2003, from, www.dese.state.mo.us/divvoced/facs_curriculum.htm

National Foundation for Educational Research (NFER). (2005). About NFER. Retrieved August 13, 2005, from http://www.nfer.ac.uk/about-nfer/

National Research Council. (2002). *Scientific research in education*. Washington, DC: National Academic Press.

National Research Council. (2005). *Advancing scientific research in education*. Washington, DC: National Academies Press.

Nias, J. (1993). Primary teachers talking: A reflexive account of longitudinal research. In: M. Hammersley (Ed.), *Educational research: Current issues*. London: Paul Chapman with the Open University.

No Child Left Behind (NCLB). (2000). Retrieved March 16, 2004, from http://www.ed.gov/nclb/methods/index.html?src = ov

Noddings, N. (2004). War, critical thinking, and self-understanding. *Phi Delta Kappan*, Spring, 489–495.

Ontario Ministry of Education. (1998). *Literacy in Ontario: The rewards are for life*. Toronto, ONT: Author.

Ontario Ministry of Education. (2005). *The Ontario curriculum grades 9 and 10: Canadian and world studies*. Toronto, ONT: Author.

Palmer, P. (1993). *Promises of paradox*. London: Potters House.

Phillips, D. C. (2005). The contested nature of empirical education research (and why philosophy of education offers little help). *Journal of Philosophy of Education, 39*(4), 576–597.

Plato. (1973). *The republic*. New York: Arno Press.

Popper, K. (2002). *The logic of scientific discovery*. London: Routledge.

Postman, N. (1988). *Conscientious objections: Stirring up trouble about language, technology and education*. New York: Knopf.

Pratt, D. (1994). *Curriculum planning: A handbook for professionals*. Orlando, FL: Harcourt Brace.

Quay, L. C. (1971). Language, dialect, test performance of Negro children. *Child Development, 42*, 5–15.

Quine, W. V. O. (1951). Two dogmas of empiricism. *The Philosophical Review, 60,* 20–43.

Ravitch, D. (2000). *Left back: A century of failed school reforms.* New York: Simon & Schuster.

Remmling, G. W. (1973). *Towards the sociology of knowledge*: Origin and development of a sociological thought style. London: Routledge and Kegan Paul.

Ricoeur, P. (1967). *Fallible man.* Chicago, IL: Henry Regenery.

Ricoeur, P. (1978). *Main trends of research in social and human sciences.* New York: Mouton/UNESCO.

Rousseau, J. J. (1974). *Emile.* London: Dent.

Sadker, M. & Sadker, D. (1995). *Failing at fairness: How our schools cheat girls.* New York: Scribner.

Sadovnik, A., Cookson, P. W., & Semel, S. F. (2001). *Exploring education: An introduction into the foundations of education.* Boston, MA: Allyn & Bacon.

Sanders, J. T. (1978). Teacher effectiveness: Accepting the null hypothesis. *Journal of Educational Thought, 12*(3), 184–189.

Sartre, J. P. (1960). *The transcendence of the ego: An existentialist theory of consciousness.* Washington, DC: The Noonday Press.

Saul, J. R. (1995). The unconscious civilization. Toronto, ON: House of Anansi Press.

Scheurich, J. J. (1997). *Research method in the postmodern.* London/Washington, DC: Falmer Press.

Schwandt, T. (2005). A diagnostic reading of scientifically based research for education. *Educational Theory, 55*(3), 285–305.

Searle, J. R. (1995). *The construction of social reality.* New York: Free Press.

Smedslund, J. (1979). Between the analytic and arbitrary: A case study of psychological research. *Scandinavian Journal of Psychology, 20,* 129–140.

Social Sciences and Humanities Research Council of Canada. (2005). *Knowledge council: SSHRC, 2006–2011.* Ottawa, Canada: Author.

Spencer, H. (1928). *Essays on education, etc. Introduction by C. W. Eliot.* London: Dent.

Sroufe, G. E. (1997). Improving the "awful reputation" of education research. *Educational Researcher, 26*(1), 26–28.

St. Pierre, E. A. (2006). Scientifically based research in education: Epistemology and ethics. *Adult Education Quarterly, 56*(4), 238–266.

Stumpf, S. E. (1989). *Philosophy: History and problems.* New York: McGraw-Hill.

Suzuki, D. (2005). *David Suzuki: The autobiography.* Vancouver, BC: Greystone Books.

Tanner, D. & Tanner, L. N. (1980). *Curriculum development : Theory into practice.* New York: Macmillan.

Taylor, C. (1971). Interpretation and the sciences of man. *The Review of Metaphysics, 25*(1): 3–51.

The World Bank. (2004). Lifelong learning in ECA. Retrieved October 18, 2004, from http://wbln0018. worldbank.org/ECA/ECSHD.nsf/ExtECADocByUnid/4887D2EA0F2834EF85256 D81005D0560?Opendocument

Thorndike, E. L. (1898). Animal intelligence: An experimental study of the associative processes in animals. *Psychological Review Monograph Supplement, 2*(4), 1–109.

Weber, M. (1991). Value judgments in social science. In: R. Boyd, P. Gasper, & J. D. Trout (Eds.). *Philosophy of science.* Cambridge, MA: MIT Press.

Wertsch, J. V. (1998). *Mind as action.* Oxford: Oxford University Press.

Winch, P. (1966). *The idea of a social science and its relation to philosophy.* London: Routledge.

Winzer, M. (2001). *Children with exceptionalities in Canadian classrooms.* Toronto, ONT: Pearson Education Canada.

Wittgenstein, L. (1963). *Philosophical investigations.* Trans. G. E. M. Anscombe. Oxford: Blackwell.

Wittgenstein, L. (1975). *Tractatus logico-philosophicus.* London: Routledge & Kegan Paul.

Woolfolk, A., Winne, P., & Perry, N. (2005). *Educational psychology.* Toronto, ONT: Pearson Education Canada.

Name Index

Subject Index

Printed in the United States
97832LV00003B/322-336/A